HOSPITAL STRIKE
Women, Unions, and Public Sector Conflict

HOSPITAL STRIKE

Women, Unions, and Public Sector Conflict

JERRY P. WHITE
University of Western Ontario

Thompson Educational Publishing, Inc.
Toronto

Requests for permission to make copies of any part of the work should
be mailed to: Thompson Educational Publishing, Inc., 11 Briarcroft Road,
Toronto, Ontario, Canada M6S 1H3

Canadian Cataloguing in Publication Data

White, Jerry Patrick, 1951-
    Hospital strike

Includes bibliographical references.
ISBN 1-55077-006-3

1. Hospital Strike, Ontario, 1981. 2. Strikes and lockouts - Hospitals -
Ontario. 3. Canadian Union of Public Employees. 4. Women in
trade-unions - Ontario. I. Title.

RA971.35.W45 1990   331.89'28136211'09713   C90-093687-8

ISBN 1-55077-006-3
Printed in Canada.
1 2 3 4 5   94 93 92 91 90

Table of Contents

Acknowledgements

I would like to thank Carl Cuneo for his many comments and suggestions during the drafts of this work. I would also like to thank Pat Armstrong, Jack Richardson, Bill Coleman, Hugh Armstrong, and Linda Frank for their help along the way.

To the members of the Canadian Union of Public Employees—a personal thank you for your support, energy, and time. A special thanks to Gil Levine, Paul Barry, Annette Gibson, Peter Douglas, Julie Davis, Jane Stinson, Judy Darcy, Grace Hartman, and the many, many other unionists who took extra time to help me.

A special thanks to my dear family Christine, Kelly, and Diane; my mother, Mary; Doug and Grace.

Preface

Since World War II Western economies have changed dramatically. The traditional blue collar production plants and primary industries where men marched to work, where unions were built, and where strikers basked in glories or buckled in defeat have given way. The service, finance, and retail sectors have come to ascendancy. Where men stood for pay packets we find women in equal numbers. Where "brotherhoods" described the gender composition of their unions now women represent more than a third of the members.

Despite these changes we are slow to change our research agendas because we are still learning a great deal from the important studies of male-dominated blue collar industries—whether from Benyon's car workers, Blauner's typesetters, Buroway's engine plants, the auto workers of Eric Batstone's work or the sweeping views of Braverman.

However, we now have a challenge to understand the new work arrangements in fresh and innovative ways. We have a more public sector, more white collar, more female work world. Many (such as Thompson 1985 and Beechy 1982) point out that the differences between women and men at work, in conflict and in change, have not been adequately explored by the theory and empirical studies to date. Boreham (1986; 188–89) has chastised us for ignoring wider political economy, the accumulation crisis for example, in our examination of labour process. Eric Batstone (1987; 26) charges much of labour process research with being reductionist and simply "reading" capital's strategies in light of an unidirectional desire to control labour.

This study endeavours to contribute theory and evidence towards alleviating the deficiencies in our research to date. It sympathetically challenges leading conflict theories, particularly Braverman, and the related labour process approaches.

In 1981 the Canadian Union of Public Employees (CUPE) staged a strike in Ontario Hospitals. This is an exploratory case study of the causes and effects of that strike. The study looks in depth at the hospitals of Greater Hamilton and Burlington and draws on the peoples' experiences and archival records from across the Province of Ontario, Canada. This strike provides the opportunity to assess the role of political environment, union structure and action, and gender in creating and sustaining the conditions for strike action in the public sector.

This book is timely. The recent "crisis" in the hospitals with nurses' strikes, bed shortages, and labour shortfalls can be traced back to the same fiscal difficulties that are outlined in this volume. We trace how labour legislation and the fiscal policies of the federal and provincial governments had an impact on hospitals and their workers. Fiscal policy changes that began in the federal-provincial conferences on cost sharing are tracked through to the strike. Labour legislation in the hospital sector destroyed collective bargaining at a time when labour process changes, unpopular with the workers, were taking place in the hospital.

The majority of hospital workers in 1981 were women. The study pursues, through interviews and archival data, the links between gender and the decision to strike. Also the strike had repercussions for the union and for women hospital workers. In addition, it had wider political consequences, such as the undermining of existing labour legislation.

The book challenges many assumptions previously held about work, the labour process, and gender. It ties together aspects of political economy with gender and organizational behaviour and in so doing raises many questions.

The passing of free trade legislation will weigh heavily on the hospitals in our country. It will lead to an attempt to intensify the labour process and in so doing will put a strain on labour and industrial relations. If the agreement creates the atmosphere for privatization, then the hospitals might well become a battle ground for labour and management and labour and government.

I can only hope this sparks debate and further research into labour process and the public sector.

Jerry White

1

Labour Process: Introducing the Debates

In 1981 the Canadian Union of Public Employees (CUPE) staged a hospital strike in Ontario. In many ways this appeared to be an exceptional action. Standard industrial relations models offered few insights into the causes of the conflict. Macro-level indicators, such as unemployment levels, pointed away from strike action (see Anderson 1981). Here was a workplace dominated by women workers. There was no right to strike in Ontario hospitals and many of the union leaders did not support the action.

These circumstances led many analysts to suggest the strike was an aberration and too unique to provide us with any insights or understandings. As a result, this conflict has remained a mystery.

Several "popular" theories of the strike were constructed by some of the major participants. The Ontario Hospital Association (OHA) stated that the strike was engineered by a conspiracy of union leaders. The "hospital workers were manipulated and stage managed," according to some OHA members. The Government publicly attached responsibility to "people seeking martyrdom." According to this theory, union members were "swept away" and "misled by union leaders" who did not serve the interests of their members (McMurtry 1981). Senior union negotiators claimed that the strike occurred because of the manipulation of a small group of radicals and leftists—a "core of persons" who "wanted to go to war" and "change the system."

These "agitator theories" have little explanatory power and they divert attention away from failings in legislation, general labour relations and growing problems in the functioning of hospitals in Ontario, and problems in the union. An initial investigation into the strike revealed that the change in the labour process in the hospitals played an important part in promoting the strike, particularly for the women hospital workers.

This study uses elements of the labour process framework to evaluate the hospital workers' strike. It also provides a basis for broader issues and debates about the labour process. In 1974 Harry Braverman reopened this long neglected area of investigation and controversy. In his *Labour and Monopoly Capital* (1974), he made an perceptive attempt to study the changing nature of work over the last 100 years. While Braverman has received much well-deserved praise, there has been a consistency and cogency to the criticisms.

Scholars have identified three areas of weakness where the relationship between labour process and resistance by workers has been ignored by Braverman. These include: (1) the relationship of workers' unions to resistance and the labour process; (2) the role of gender (conditioned by the relationship between home and paid workplace); and, (3) the role of the state and the fiscal crisis. Critics have called for empirical studies to look at these three areas of perceived weakness.

The 1981 strike provides an excellent opportunity for looking at these factors. The action is by definition an act of resistance and, as we will see, allows us to look at the range of variables mentioned above. These are variables that have been left out of both traditional industrial relations and many modern labour process studies.

THE STRIKE

At midnight, January 25, 1981 the Ontario hospital strike began. Within 36 hours, more than 10,000 workers from 50 of the 65 hospitals organized by the Canadian Union of Public Employees were participating in an *illegal* strike. The strikers included housekeepers, food handlers, nursing assistants, maintenance workers, laboratory technologists, orderlies and porters. Impasses in bargaining were supposed to be passed to an arbitrator under a procedure set by the *Hospital Labour Disputes Arbitration Act* (HLDAA) of 1965. Whereas doctors could strike, the absence of the non-professional service worker would, according to the authorities, endanger public health.

The strike was unusual in many ways. In the fall of 1980, CUPE's negotiators had signed a tentative agreement with the Ontario Hospital Association. This agreement was put to the members for ratification and the hospital workers were encouraged to accept it. Despite this encouragement, the members voted 91% to reject the agreement.

CUPE staff members who had negotiated the contract, and many middle- and upper-level CUPE leaders, counselled against strike action. The government launched a publicity campaign against the strike and tried to deter strike action through intimidation. These actions succeeded with some workers but did not stop the strike.

There had been little support for the strike within the official structures of the union. As a result, there was virtually no formal organization for it. This meant that the strike depended primarily on the determination of the rank and file members. With virtually no formal organization for the strike, the province-wide action collapsed after ten days. This collapse was precipitated when hospital workers in Toronto began returning to work. In the aftermath of the strike both Government and employers took reprisals: 3,400 workers were suspended—some for up to one year; thirty-four people were fired outright; and, three senior union leaders received jail sentences.

The strike and its consequences prompted the Canadian Union of Public Employees (CUPE) to enter a period of self-examination. This resulted in two reports on the causes of problems in the union's hospital jurisdiction and collective bargaining. The long-term outcome was an internal reorganization of CUPE in the hospital sector, including the formation of an intermediate body in the Ontario District called the Ontario Council of Hospital Unions (OCHU). This Council brought together all the local unions of CUPE in the hospital sector.

Later in 1981, the original tentative agreement with slightly improved wages was imposed by an arbitrator. This was the same agreement that the rank and file unionists had originally rejected. Since 1981 there have been three rounds of negotiations. The 1983 round ended in a negotiated settlement that workers claim is one of the best ever. The 1985–86 round had to go to arbitration, as did the 1987 negotiations.

LABOUR PROCESS AND THE DEBATE WITH BRAVERMAN

What is the Labour Process?

We can see from the description of the strike that it is an action that is not easy to explain. An exploration of labour process changes in the workplace is useful in unravelling some of the causal factors. On the one hand, the labour process approach is a dynamic and useful pro-

cedure to develop explanations for the strike. On the other hand, the
strike provides, as we shall see, a framework for exploring and resolving debates within the labour process approach itself.

It was Karl Marx who introduced the concept of "labour process"
as an element of analysis. In *Capital* (Vol. 1) Marx notes that the labour process consists of "...first purposive activity, or labour itself;
secondly, its subject matter; and thirdly its instruments.... In the labour process therefore, man's activity, with the help of the instruments
of labour, brings about changes in the subject matter of labour..."
(Marx 1967: 170, 173). The subject matter is that which is being
worked on and the instruments are "things which the worker inter-
poses between himself and the subject matter of his labour, and one
which serves as the conductor of his activity." (Ibid.,171). These are
tools and methods of work.

This is not all there is to the analysis of the labour process. Marx
saw the labour process in the light of his general notions of human
nature and human needs.

> What happens is not merely that the worker brings about a change
> of form in natural objects; at the same time, in the nature that exists
> apart from himself, he realizes his own purpose...The less attractive
> he finds the work in itself, the less congenial the method of work,
> the less he enjoys it as something which gives scope to his bodily
> and mental powers... (Marx 1967, 170)

For Marx, the labour process is the *human activity of production*. It
differs qualitatively from the instinctually-driven work of animals.
The work of humans, carried out in a labour process, is purposive,
conscious, and conceptual. In Marx's earlier writings, such as the
Economic and Philosophic Manuscripts of 1844, there is more emphasis
on human nature, personal growth, and the consciousness that takes
place in the context of work (Marx 1964, 139). In later works, such as
Capital, Marx concentrates on the structural determinants and general
patterns that characterize the production processes. Even with this
emphasis on structure we can see the continuing acknowledgement
of the interaction between personal attitudes and consciousness and
structural determinants. This study follows in this tradition. It examines the labour process in its widest sense, as well as the questions of
changing attitudes and consciousness.

People develop relations within their work world. These relations
have three dimensions:

(1) Social relations: People form relationships at the social level
when they are in continuing contact with each other, as in workpla-

ces. The relations are characterized by "shared values, intimacy and a partial [workplace] culture" (Salaman 1986: 31–32).

(2) Normative Component: People share "values, norms and knowledge" (Ibid., 32).

(3) Personal Identity: People develop a portion of their identity of self in the labour process and the interactions defined by it. These are interactions between fellow workers and with the environment.

These aspects are conditioned by several factors. First is the expectations, ideas, and understandings people bring with them into the job. Second, the process itself conditions attitudes and self identity. Third, forces outside of the workplace, such as the business cycle, condition the entire process.

Many studies have noted that change breeds resistance (Penn 1982; Blauner 1964; Burawoy 1979; Friedman 1977). The forms of resistance are many. Some people will absent themselves, some will sabotage, and some will strike. The external considerations may influence the selection of tactics. The labour market and business cycle, according to some theories, will discourage a strike if they are on a downturn. Sometimes, altering the labour process significantly diminishes the quality of work. Goldthorpe (1968), for example, found that some workers respond in an instrumental fashion: they demand a payment for the undesirable, monotonous, and uncreative environment in which they work. Other workers may react differently. As Thompson (1983: 185) has noted, Goldthorpe ignored women in the study of rewards. In our study, gender differences are of particular importance because the men did act instrumentally but the women did not.

Others, such as Blauner (1964), argue that people do not work for external (extrinsic) rewards alone. People are seen as having a need and drive to fulfill themselves through work. The fulfillment, or realization of one's nature, comes from working productively (Marx 1967). Fox (1980: 178–79) notes:

> When men (*sic*) strike for higher pay the passion of their campaign may sometimes be strengthened by resentment against intrinsic deprivations...those demands may not be articulated if only because in our society men are expected to strike for pay.

People bring ideas and consciousness to the work process. These understandings determine, to a degree, what they want and get out of their work. In working, people are changed. Their ideas, attitudes and feelings are slowly and subtly transformed as they confront the environment of men, women, the law and the circumstances of their working world. This is an extension of what Marx (*Capital* Vol.I) meant when he said that as we transform nature we transform ourselves. Modifications in the labour process disrupt the systems of evolving change, and this affects the people involved and can create resistance such as a strike.

The Debates

The current debate over the nature of the labour process was kindled by the 1974 publication of Braverman's *Labour and Monopoly Capital*. There was subsequently a flood of both supportive and critical research. Many excellent summaries of Braverman's work exist (see Littler 1982b, Wood 1982). Essentially, Braverman argued that the monopoly stage of capitalism demanded the proliferation of a management strategy that would make workers increasingly interchangeable and relatively passive. Scientific management was that vehicle. Scientific management, or "Taylorism" as it is often called, deskills work through a detailed division of labour and automated technologies. Taylor's program divided work into more and more sub-routines that required a reduced skill level. This made the workers doing those jobs replaceable and reduced labour's power vis-à-vis capital. The scientific management system changed the labour process by fragmenting tasks, allowing the introduction of automated technologies and a system of close, detailed, and authoritarian supervision. This affected workers' attitudes to their labours by taking away many creative aspects from work (see Braverman 1974, Zimbalist 1982). Braverman saw this Taylorist management system as the vehicle for the deskilling of the working class.

The simplicity of the argument is both its strength and weakness. Braverman's characterization of the "fourth" stage of capitalist development as a logical extension of Marx's three stages (simple cooperation, manufacture, and machinofacture) captured people's interest. This stage of monopoly capitalism involved a homogenization of the working class through deskilling and a subordination of the working class. This challenged the leading functionalist interpretations based on Emile Durkheim's *Division of Labour*. Durkheim had reasoned that new technology would lead to increased skill levels and greater differentiation in the working class.

The critique of this general deskilling thesis has taken different forms. Daniel Bell (1973), on the one hand, supports Durkheim's contentions and refuses to recognize job loss and deskilling. He sees an

extension of skills as a logical and inevitable consequence of technological advancement. On the other hand, British Weberians and neo-
Marxists have taken issue with Braverman selectively. They point out
that different amounts of deskilling occur in different economic sectors. Some see the deskilling of the craftsman that Braverman notes in
his thesis and some do not. Different national experiences and different gender experiences have also been pointed out (see Beechy 1983;
Burawoy 1978; Coombs 1978; Thompson 1983; Wood 1982). The criticism of Braverman's thesis that it overestimates the extent of scientific management and deskilling is not explored in this work. A
discussion of these issues is contained in several of the many theoreti-
cal/empirical critiques such as Elger (1982, 1979), Penn (1982), and
Crompton and Reid (1982).

The Criticisms of Braverman

One major criticism of Braverman's thesis is his underestimation of
the resistance that workers show to changes in the labour process.

A second criticism is that Braverman does not treat gender in the
context of the relationship between home (family) and the paid labour force. He ignores women's consciousness with regards to the
labour process.

The third criticism of Braverman is that his theory fails to take into
account the role of the various levels of government and state bureaucracy. Management decisions on changing the conditions of work are
conditioned by the political and economic environment created by
the actions of different levels of the government.

These three criticisms are addressed in our case study of hospital
workers.

Critique One: The Context of Resistance

Braverman sees the working class as passive, inert, and accepting
of the degradation of work.

> Indeed, one of the main criticisms that has been leveled at Braver-
> man is his rendering of the working class as passive, inert, living in
> accordance with the forces which act on it (Wood 1982: 15).

Employing the classic Marxist dichotomy, he sets as his task the description of "a class in itself," not "a class for itself." Thus, he avoids
describing how the working class, "for itself," resists changes in
work. Implicit in Braverman's analysis of the passivity of the working
class is a presupposition that the organizations of workers will not

mount a resistance to labour process changes. As we will see, there were some union officials who did wish to accept forced changes in the hospital; however, the workers themselves did not.

Critique Two: Gender: Production, Reproduction, Consciousness and Resistance; a Braverman Blindspot

Braverman has been congratulated for looking at women as workers and has "fully incorporated this understanding into his analysis" (Baxandall *et al.* 1976; see also Beechy 1982). However, his concentration on continuous-process, wage labour work, and his splitting of the discussion of women and family off to the sphere of consumption, creates a void in his analysis. He does not examine the effect and interaction of home and paid labour market on women as workers. Beechy (1982: 54–73) notes two sets of feminist criticisms that have been made. One set criticises Braverman "...for failing to analyze the ways in which monopoly capitalism has affected the domestic role of women as housewives" since "...women's specific location in the family *and* the labour process affects their consciousness" (Beechy 1982: 54). The second type of critique questions the applicability of the wholesale application of Braverman's wage-labour production-industry models. In workplaces where women are concentrated the circumstances are more complex with regards to deskilling and the creation of a "reserve army of labour."

Braverman does not ignore the family but centres his analysis on the transfer of goods production from the family to the "universal market." Clothing, and other such needs, once produced for use in the family setting, are now produced for sale to workers. This transfer of production means the family "...retains the sole function of being an institution for the consumption of commodities (Beechy 1982: 57). Women then "move from producing use values within the domestic economy to producing them as...wage labourer[s]..." (ibid.) As women are drawn into the labour force because of this shift in production, and the inability of working families to survive on one wage, they become an industrial "reserve army of labour."

While Braverman argues that women constitute a reserve army and tend to enter low-wage occupations, he does not explain why or how. (This problem will be explored in Chapter 4.)

Braverman extends his analysis of the deskilling of labour to include women. Women as "domestic craftspersons" are deskilled through the transfer of "productive" work out of the home. In the work force outside the household, women take up both deskilled jobs (i.e. jobs that are degraded through the detailed division of labour) in industry and newly-expanding "feminized" jobs such as clerical work and service. Critics point out that some work is "feminized" as women are brought into the labour force (e.g. teaching) and some are newly created or recreated before women are moved in (e.g. clerical). This debate has only peripheral application to this study and will only be touched on in passing.

This study explores the linkages between women's role in the family and the paid labour force. In addition, we look at women's place in unions as a result of this link between home and paid labour. Both sets of relations are placed in the context of resistance to the changing labour process.

Critique Three: The State and its Relation to Work and Strikes

A third general criticism of Braverman's thesis relates to his treatment (or lack of it) of the relationship between class relations and state institutions. Elger (1982) argues that Braverman fails to analyze the actions of the state apparatus that affect on the general conditions of work. Such an analysis would be even more important in public sector workplaces where state involvement is, by definition, more pronounced. The increasing role of the public sector in the economic life of advanced capitalist economies makes this an even more important consideration.

A second area of criticism related to the state pertains to the fiscal crisis. "There is little indication [by Braverman] of the manner in which...[management strategies] and related initiatives arose out of any crisis in the process of accumulation" (Elger: 1982: 41). The problems of the fiscal crisis of the state, the effect this has had on the organization of work, and types of resistance displayed by workers receive no mention by Braverman.

This study looks at how the state's fiscal crisis affects work in the public sector and evaluates its effect on the 1981 hospital workers' strike.

WORKING PROPOSITIONS

We noted above that an initial investigation of the strike revealed that labour process changes had taken place in the period leading up to the strike. Given these indications, and others concerning budgetary changes, a set of hypotheses could be constructed for evaluation. However, as this is an exploratory case study, it is not a good vehicle for hypothesis testing. It is preferable to work with a set of propositions that have some explanatory power. The propositions below were derived from information gathered during the initial assessment of the feasibility of the study.

Proposition One

It is proposed that the changes in the labour process impelled hospital workers to take action in order to safeguard their appreciated sense of the job. That is to say, the workers struck because the complex set of rewards they gained from work was being eroded through labour process changes. There was a gender specific response where women perceived a need to stop this erosion and men expressed a need to increase compensation for the changes.

Proposition Two

Politics and economics in the country played an important role in creating the conditions for the strike. The federal and provincial levels of government, in trying to deal with an on-going fiscal crisis, embarked on a series of measures to weaken the union, distort collective bargaining, and worsen working conditions. These problems frustrated hospital workers who felt compelled to take the option of the illegal strike.

Proposition Three

The organization, structure, and functioning of the union contributed to the decision to strike. There was a perceived lack of a decision-making ability, excessive centralization, and infighting among leadership levels. All contributed to the workers disagreeing with the leadership proposals and forced a confrontation with the management and the Ontario government.

Proposition Four

The strike precipitated a union reorganization that benefited workers. It brought pride to the hospital workers and slowed the deterioration of the labour process. It was not successful in reversing changes in the labour process nor did the strike secure any exceptional compensation for the workers.

The following outline shows how data was collected to enable an examination of these propositions.

OUTLINE OF THE BOOK

This study was based on extensive archival and interview material. Archival material was collected across the province, while interviews were largely restricted to the area of Hamilton, Ontario, and the central offices of CUPE and the OHA.

In Chapter 2 we explore the fiscal crisis and how the measures to meet the crisis altered the industrial relations in the hospital sector.

Chapter 3 explores why women work and what they want from work, how the changes in the organization and processes of work affect them, the role of unions in women's working lives, and problems they experience taking part in their unions. Common assertions about women and collective action are examined and an explanation of why women voted for, and participated in, the strike is offered. The chapter contrasts the attitudes of male and female hospital workers with respect to work and their reasons for striking.

With the context set, we move on to an exploration of the strike itself in Chapter 4. The events leading up to the strike, the process of the strike, and its demise are chronicled. The union's problems are highlighted and the workers' view of the need to strike is explained.

Chapter 5, *The Aftermath*, concentrates on the effects of the strike. We discuss the changes that came to the union and to the negotiating process. Themes initiated earlier are continued. These include, among others, changes for women in the union, the legislation forcing arbitration, and the denial of the right to strike.

The book ends with a chapter that draws some conclusions from our findings.

2

The State, Fiscal Crisis Management And The Shape Of Labour Relations

To unravel the complexity of the 1981 strike many elements must be considered. When labour and capital engage in free collective bargaining, the state plays an important role in setting the conditions for the bargaining. *The Ontario Labour Relations Act*, the fiat of the labour relations board, and general labour law constrain the participants in the bargaining process. They alter the actions, change the attitudes, and play an important role in shaping industrial relations. Where there is no "free" collective bargaining and no freedom to withdraw labour, the state's influence is even more pronounced. In the case at hand, both bargaining and general labour relations were quite distorted.

To understand the roots of conflict in the hospital sector one must understand how the state influences industrial relations. The factors examined in this chapter are not restricted to those elements connected directly with law. We will also be analyzing changes in the economy and the measures taken to combat crisis situations. As well, the effect of arbitration legislation on the functioning of union democracy will be reviewed. All of these elements affect the evolution of relations between management and labour and will help us to explain the strike by the hospital workers.

In 1971 Frank Isbester concluded from his study of the Ontario hospital system:

> The causal factors of the unions' nascent struggle are the inter-relationships among wage levels, governmental wage control, compulsory arbitration, and the prohibition of the right to strike...

> If the present bargaining environment is maintained, the implications of wage ceilings, compulsory arbitration, and prohibition of strike action may be expected to result in a large number of illegal

strikes, one-day work stoppages, rotating strikes, and slow-downs designed to inconvenience hospital management, while maintaining essential patient care facilities (Isbester 1971: 348–349).

In his recommendations, delivered to a health-care conference in Hamilton, Isbester advocated many changes in the system of industrial relations in the Ontario hospital sector. These changes included restoring the right to strike and ending government interference in setting or controlling wages in the hospitals.

Multiple rounds of legislated and informal wage controls, threatened strikes, and a massive "illegal" walkout marked the decade after Isbester's study. We hope to show that the state has largely determined the way industrial relations have developed in the quasi-public hospital sector, setting and enforcing the field of action for collective bargaining and other related interactions between capital and labour. At the same time, changes in the labour process led to a subsequent drop in health-care quality.

THE NATURE OF THE FISCAL CRISIS

The economic recession in the 1970s brought demands on the Canadian state at both the provincial and federal levels. As Panitch (1985: 264) pointed out, the state's general response to the economic crisis was to develop new subsidies for the corporate sector. This implied a shift of burden to the employed worker.[1] While this shift was occurring, the inflation rate was quite high (see Table 2.1). The inflation rate that had ballooned in the early 1970s pushed unionized workers to seek substantial wage increases. There were many strikes and some major wage increases (see Tables 2.2 and 2.3).

There are trends evident in the data. Table 2.1 shows a substantial increase (approximately 46%) in the *rate* of inflation from 1970 to 1972 and a further 125% increase from 1972 to 1974. During the same period the number of strikes suggests a delayed reaction to this high inflation. This is because union members were tied into agreements for one, two, and three years. There is a considerable increase in strike

---

[1] In calculating tax sources there are two aspects to the income tax based pool: the personal and the corporate. The subsidization of corporate interests implies a shift of the tax burden to the personal income tax side.

Table 2.1: Changes in Consumer Price Index 1966–1978

Year	CPI (Base 1971=100)	Change in Annual Inflation Rate (Expressed as Average %)
1967 (average)	86.5	3.6
1968	90.0	4.0
1969	94.1	4.5
1970	97.2	3.3
1971	100.0	2.9
1972	104.8	4.8
1973	112.7	7.5
1974	125.0	10.9
1975	138.5	10.8
1976	148.9	7.5
1977	159.8	8.0
1978	174.2	9.0

SOURCE: *Canada Year Book Annual*, Table 23.8, 1985, 1975.

action during the 1972 to 1974 period (+103%), and the real wage increases (Table 2.3) indicate that gains were made up to 1976. The strikes of 1974–75 generated a substantial increase in real wages but after wage controls were introduced the drop was substantial. Wage controls were designed to cut short the movement to higher wage demands and real wage gains.

The increasing magnitude of the deficit was exacerbated by the state's moves to aid the accumulation of private capital (see Wolfe 1977). The government was active in promoting certain mega-projects and had designs on aspects of the petroleum industry. Officials had a continuing commitment to create employment through expansion of private capital investment. These and other aspects of the promotion of private capital accumulation implied that corporate taxation was not the route the government could take to reduce the fiscal crisis.

Given this, the need to maintain and enhance various programs became a burden. The typical response was to cut spending on some programs until revenues caught up. However, given the nature of current programs, it was not possible simply to cut programs as they were seen by the public as a positive and necessary part of the Canadian way of life. The public had, in Maxwell Henderson's words:

Table 2.2: Strikes and Lockouts 1967–1977

Year	Number of Strikes	% of Total Work Time
1967	522	.25
1968	582	.32
1969	595	.46
1970	542	.39
1971	569	.16
1972	598	.43
1973	667	.30
1974	1216	.46
1975	1171	.53
1976	1039	.55*
1977	803	.15

* This is artificially high due to the one day general strike organized by the Canadian Labour Congress.
SOURCE: Labour Canada, *Strikes and Lockouts*, Table 1, 1984.

"come to see the provision of health care as a state responsibility" (Henderson 1975: 141).

The state was in a classic dilemma: it was caught between its own functions of legitimation and accumulation.[1] In the health-care field the contradiction was exacerbated. There could be no perceptible reduction in service because the responsibility for medical care and its delivery had been appropriated by the state in the public's eye. The country's health had become a "social good" and a social responsibil-

---

[1] The view that the state has two basic functions has its roots in Marx's notion of the class nature of the state and its relative autonomy (as developed in *The Eighteenth Brumaire of Louis Bonaparte*). James O'Connor (1973) argues that the state in capitalist society has two central and often contradictory functions, namely, accumulation and legitimation. It must create the conditions for profitable capital accumulation in the private sector while ensuring that non-capitalist classes remain supportive of the system (i.e. find legitimacy in it).

**Table 2.3: Annual Percentage Increases in Base
Rates of Major Collective Agreements**

Year	Annual Percentage Increases in Base Rates	Net Change in Real Wages
1969	7.8	
1970	8.6	5.3
1971	7.8	4.9
1972	8.8	4.0
1973	11.0	3.5
1974	14.7	3.8
1975	19.2	8.4
1976	10.9	3.4
1977	7.9	- .1
1978	7.2	1.8
1979	8.7	- .4

SOURCE: *Canada Year Book Annual. 1969–1980.* "Major Wage Settlements." (Table numbers vary year to year.)

ity, so the state must watch for a backlash over any reductions in health coverage (see Stoddard 1985; R. Evans 1984).

This is the lesson that Ontario doctors learned in 1986. When they went on strike, they learned their "freedom to work as independent professionals" doesn't include any infringement on this social good. The "public" agreed that the state can infringe on the professionals. While the fiscal crisis was deepening with inflation and escalating deficits, organized labour was trying to regain some of its losses in real wages.

Wages in the hospital sector were substantially below community standards and significantly below the poverty line set by the Economic Council of Canada (*Globe and Mail*, April 17, 1969: 1). According to the *Globe and Mail* wages were so poor that employees were leaving the hospital "in droves." Riverdale Hospital in Toronto, for example, issued 1300 income tax receipts in 1971 for a staff of only 700. Wage differentials had also increased between those inside the hospital and similar outside occupations. "The average differential between municipal labour rates and base male hospital rates was

$24.05/week in 1964. By 1972 the differential had risen to $47.51/week" (CUPE 1971: 3).

In 1973–74, hospital workers fought for and won a substantial wage increase. This brought their low wages closer to those in the outside world (Kruger 1985). The movement to bring wages in line with the outside came to a head with the 1974 Toronto settlement. The Toronto hospitals bargained as a group, threatened a walkout, and at the last minute won a $1.50/hour increase (which represented a 50% increase in many classifications). They achieved this by the unions forcing the provincial government directly into the negotiations (Kruger 1985: 57). The threat of a strike was employed as a lever and a deal was struck.

In retrospect, it may appear odd that the union could defeat the Ontario Hospital Association (OHA) in 1974 but lose badly in 1981. Poor organization on the management side in 1974 contributed to the union's ability to secure the substantial increases. In 1974, the OHA had no special bureau for handling negotiations. The Employee Relations Bureau was set up two years later. The former head of the section that dealt with CUPE, George Campbell, believes the strike threat of 1974 had more impact on the individual OHA member hospitals because of their lack of expertise than it would have had on a more sophisticated industrial relations group. The strike threat was a lever in 1974 but by 1981 it was not as cogent a weapon due to changes on the management side. Campbell adds that "They [the hospital workers] probably thought it [the strike threat] was going to work again but we could not let it influence us. We *couldn't*, it would reflect on our entire organization" (Interview, February, 1986). Thus, the 1974 union victory influenced the events of 1981.

While hospital workers were trying to narrow wage differentials with the non-hospital employees, the government was looking at the gaps between revenue on the one hand and escalating costs on the other. Since the early 1970s, cost reduction and control had become the central issue for health economists (see Manga 1983; Stoddard 1984; 1985). Government studies indicated that between 1954 and 1971, health-care expenditures accounted for approximately 30% of the total growth of government expenditures when taken as a proportion of Canada's gross national expenditure (Mustard Report: 1982).

Studies in the early 1970s predicted an upturn in costs in the 1980s due to an aging population. On top of this, projections indicated that a population bubble was moving into the more extreme cost categories of older age. The demographic trends to an older population implied a sizable increase in acute and chronic care costs (Mustard 1982; Ontario 1981). At the same time, the ability to pay was diminishing due to government deficits (Stoddard 1984: 9). This affected more than the health care sector (Panitch 1985 and Swartz 1977). The health sector costs, which represented over 30% of the provincial budget, had to be contained, but which portion and how? (see Government of Ontario, 1982). The hospitals were singled out. They account for 85% of the health costs. Within the hospitals, labour costs of medical delivery represent 75% to 80% of the total on-going expenditure. Art Kruger reflected the views of the government: "Any program of cost control is doomed without measures to cut labour cost" (Kruger 1985: 57).

The most vulnerable component of labour cost were the non-professionals, the group Torrance (1977) called the "underside" of the hospital. Other areas, such as doctors' fees, were, and remain, outside any direct control because the shape of the delivery of medicine is considered to be non-negotiable. While the Government was calling for cost restraint, the doctors were reorganizing their practices to recover even more money in payments (Evans 1984). This was possible because, in the hospitals, the physicians determined costs by the way they practice, i.e. which tests or therapies were ordered. The most expensive instrument in a hospital was and is often the doctor's pen. As a hospital administrator pointed out in an interview:

> You don't want to get into an argument with the chief of medicine over how to practice…Costs are not their concern.

Thus, the costs vulnerable to restraint were the constituency represented by the unions, such as CUPE, the Service Employees International Union (SEIU) and the Ontario Public Service Employees Union (OPSEU).

Different pressures existed for legitimation and accumulation at the different levels of government. The federal government foresaw continuing and ever-increasing transfer payments for health care. The governments were facing "sizable structural deficits" that had been "unresponsive to policy actions" designed to reduce them (Government of Canada 1983: iii). This was compounded by an erroneous projection of costs in the first place (McKeough 1975: 14). Faced with this, Ottawa decided to transfer the remaining fiscal responsibility for health care to the provinces. At the same time, the federal government moved to reduce labour's bargaining power through wage controls.

The provinces, for their part, began squeezing hospitals in the budgeting process (along with a range of other actions). Dennis Timbrell, the then-Minister of Health for Ontario, summed up the new attitude:

> From now until at least the early 1980s, one concern will override all others, for my Ministry: a determination to contain health-care costs. We are shifting some responsibilities and resources from provincial institutions to local communities...rationalizing the deployment of manpower. We are cutting back on facilities wherever they are found to exceed actual needs, and are trying hard to educate people to take greater responsibility for their health (Timbrell 1977: 37).

We will explore these changes in detail.

FEDERAL FISCAL POLICY AND ITS CONSEQUENCES

The idea of transferring aspects of the fiscal crisis from the federal to the provincial level is not new. This has happened repeatedly in economically bad times over the last 50 years. In this case, the federal government wished to change its cost-sharing program. The provinces have always had the responsibility for health care delivery. But with the 50% cost-sharing programs (and the grant system), the federal level has had to pay a lot of the costs. The process left the federal government with a large bill that increased as the *provinces* made spending decisions. The Prime Minister, Pierre Trudeau, made it clear in 1976 that the Federal Government was not prepared to carry the expense of provincial decisions (Trudeau 1976). Prior to these ministerial comments, the federal government had taken steps to make the existing cost-sharing programs somewhat unpalatable.

In the 1970s the federal government initiated talks to change the cost-sharing transfer process. The outcome came to be known as the EPF (Established Program Financing) agreement. Essentially this was a transfer of responsibilities for programs to the provinces, cancellation of cost-sharing agreements and the initiation of a fixed-sum annual transfer with few strings attached to it.

Dollars for hospital financing represented over half of the transfers by the mid-1970s. The Trudeau Government had warned the provinces that transfers for this program, medicare, and aspects of secondary education were to be terminated at the earliest possible date (Saskatchewan 1976; Carter 1977; see also Ontario Economic Council 1979). The provinces had always been justifiably skeptical of the benefit of a move like this. Years before, an Ontario Premier had noted:

> ...any federal proposal to transfer total responsibility for developed programs in exchange for additional taxation capacity and lump sum payment...offers no real gain for the provinces (Federal Provincial Tax Structure Report: 1966).

The provinces recognized the potential for program costs to outstrip the new sources of monies (Carter 1977: 546). Despite these provincial fears, the federal government pushed forward for agreement. Trudeau cloaked the argument in legitimacy. He argued there could be a better maintenance of standards, better planning of programs, greater autonomy for the provinces, and improved democratic relations between the federal government and the provinces (Trudeau 1976). This put the reluctant provinces in an awkward position. They had many grievances with the existing programs and they knew the situation was going to get worse because the federal government was committed to getting out of the cost sharing. The appeal to these "legitimacy" issues encouraged provincial representatives to make a counter-offer. Ottawa was obliged to sweeten the deal by making the first few years' transfers greater than they were under the old agreements.

The actual agreement involved personal and corporate tax points going to the provinces and a cash payment. The provinces agreed because there had been a deterioration of funding relations due to the growing fiscal problems at the federal level (Saskatchewan Government 1976: 15). The provinces complained of problems including:

1. Unilateral imposition of ceilings on the rate of growth of federal contributions to established programs. In the June 1975 Federal budget, for example, ceilings of 14.5% for 1976–1977, 12% for 1977–1978 and 10% thereafter were imposed. This was to cost Ontario approximately $200 million over the 1976 to 1980 period (McKeough 1975: 3–5).

2. Abrupt policy switches made programs non-shareable, leaving provinces with the total bill (McKeough 1975; Saskatchewan: Social Services Briefing Notes: 1976).

3. Rigid eligibility criteria that led to "...inequities, feuds and distortions" (McKeough 1975: 5).

4. Administrative costs were too high and procedures cumbersome. The existence of federal auditors in provincial departments gave the Federal Government a window on provincial affairs.(Saskatchewan: Social Services Briefing Notes: 1976).

Other problems with the cost-shared funding arrangements included:

1. Its effect on provincial decision making, i.e. when deciding how to expand services only shareable programs were considered (Saskatchewan; 1976).

2. Indirect financial losses were incurred. A neighbourhood clinic system, for example, might be more cost effective than treatment in a hospital but if the clinic was not cost shared there is pressure to deliver the programs through a hospital (McKeough, 1975).

3. The very slow payments back to the provinces (Carter, 1977).

In addition, the rich "early years" of the new transfer program made it appealing, given provincial budget problems. These additional dollars could be diverted to solve immediate budget shortfalls in other areas. This was a short-sighted response, given that costs would outstrip transfer revenues—which did happen to a degree (Stoddard 1984 Ontario 1982: 47).

The manoeuvering around cost sharing is an interesting case study in the legitimacy/accumulation process of fiscal crisis management. The federal government picked programs to divest that were costly *and* would not need a federal presence to ensure continuation. The federal government did not want to reduce the quality of health care. It counted on the provinces not cutting back on services such as health care because this would lead to such a public uproar that it might threaten provincial legitimacy. Thus, Ottawa gained control of escalating costs while protecting its political position and the legitimacy of the process. The provinces reacted as expected. They reorganized several priorities rather than make dramatic cuts in services such as health care.

On the side of accumulation, Gonick (1976: 88–95) has argued that the aborted 1969 recession in the United States created a dramatic inflationary spiral and left labour "undisciplined" due to the "tight" labour market. The Canadian Government, according to Gonick, took the same path as the U.S. government and found the extreme inflation and wage demands of 1974–75 intolerable to capital accumulation. This led to the decision to dampen wage demands and to try to slow price increases. This was preferable to recession through restraint. The EPF program also allowed a slowing down of the increase in structural deficits, and this could be pointed to as restraint by the state.

The provincial response to this impending squeeze was to continue to tighten up the supply of funds to the hospitals. The changing fiscal arrangements, initially sweeter for the provinces, provided an impetus for restraint because "provincial expenditure functions expand faster than revenues" (Perry 1977).

While cost-sharing programs for health care were being negotiated, Ontario commissioned Maxwell Henderson to do a complete program review. The *Special Program Review* (1975) provided the basis for a tighter-fisted approach to health care financing. Henderson concluded that:

1. Deficits were going to rise markedly in the late 1970s and 1980s. These deficits would result from the contradictory movement of revenue and expenditure.

2. There would be a *decline* in the rate of increase of the Gross Provincial Product (GPP) due to economic slowdown. This slowdown would create a *greater* pressure for increased services [economic downturns lead to increased demands for social services] (Henderson 1975: 23).

The report suggested wage guidelines to reduce delivery costs.[1]

The program review made specific recommendations in the health field. Henderson proposed:

1. Productivity in the hospitals must go up among the service workers and semi-professionals (RNA and Laboratory Technicians) (Henderson 1975: 143).

---

[1] The Ontario Government enacted a series of wage restraint laws which lasted from the close of the federal wage controls until the 1980s.

2. The province should phase out as many beds as possible without jeopardizing service (ibid., 149).

3. The hospitals should be encouraged to use part-time staff and employ labour-saving technology (ibid., 150).

4. Thorough a review of operating costs in the hospitals, ascertain all possible ways of reducing the total paid hours for hospital staff (ibid., 152).

There can be little doubt that the recommendations were acted on:

> In the eight year period between 1973 and 1981 full-time hospital staff declined by nearly 5,000 positions, while part-time increased by about 13,000. The growth in part-time workers did not balance out the full-time since total paid hours of work declined by 150,000 hours (Sykes, 1982: 127).

The Ontario Economic Council commented in 1979:

> Since the early 1970s the Ministry of Health has resorted to severe measures to control costs. Many of them focused on the largest institutions...[like] hospitals. Hospitals have been closed down, a large number of beds closed, departments emptied, mergers of hospitals, staff layoffs, capital spending down, etc. (*Issues and Alternatives*, 1979 Update).

Our interviews with hospital workers touched on the dramatic move to part-time and on-call personnel:

> They have about 800 on-call in the two civics; no benefits, no fixed schedules. They are supposed to be used for sick replacement. The system is misused, people come in to cover heavy times—to substitute for full timers that are needed (Interview, Laboratory Technician, August, 1985).

There were no massive layoffs but, by not replacing staff who retired or quit, a cutback was effected:

> We can't put out a list of 30 laid off here or 50 there. They just don't replace all the people who quit or retire. I can say we are down 700 since 1972 or 1973 (Interview, Executive Member, Local 794, September, 1985).

There was also a phasing out of orderlies and cutbacks in portering. The orderlies' work was passed onto other staff.

Patients were sent home much earlier than in the past. The effect was two-fold. First, when a patient leaves, the staff perform a set routine of sterilizing, cleaning, and bedmaking. These time-consuming tasks were required more often. Second, the patients were, on average, more ill and required more care. The longer recuperation times in the past meant that there were a few days when patients required little care. This was when staff got to know patients, converse, and become friendly.

The reorganization of work was dramatic, and the consequences for efficiency, job satisfaction, and morale were equally obvious. A new element was introduced—the fear of falling standards of health-care.

> We were a family in a village before the changes. We want it back. The attitude to patients has changed. Staff can't accept that....The patient used to be king, now we are lucky if we even know anyone's name....Patients are mass produced. We had pride, things were clean, people could point to their work and say that's my work. No more—it's frustrating (Housekeeper, September 1985).

The majority of hospital workers who were in care-giving roles or close to patients (such as RNA's or housekeepers) expressed concern over deterioration of patient care. The concern with the quality of health care was an important cause of unrest, dissatisfaction, and lack of morale. The workers in hospitals had always been known to have a concern for the maintenance of patient care. This is "natural" given that it is connected to their "pride in work." The increase in part-time and attrition style layoffs meant workers could not take time off or transfer horizontally to a new job. Stress and "burnout" were on the rise.

These issues related to changes in the labour process. The link between the various levels of fiscal difficulty and labour process change was visible when management tried to intensify work in order to keep within budgetary constraints.

> At Belleville we are entering our fourth year with frozen staffing establishments despite increasing workloads. Over this period staffing has been held to December, 1971, levels (Rickard,1975: 44).

One demand in the 1981 strike was for a reduction in this increased workloading.

The provincial government embarked on a two-sided policy to deal with the fiscal crisis. The reorganization of the funding, experimenting with user charges, and other measures designed to control costs were one side of the initiative. The other side was the reduction of labour's power to interfere in this crisis management. Both the federal government (1975–1978) and Ontario tried to control wage demands. This policy curtailed expenditure on wages and it also further eroded collective bargaining. The more than six years of wage controls destroyed traditional relationships between occupations, between sectors, *and* heated up an already simmering caldron of discontent.

Wage Controls

Wage controls originated as one of a cluster of policies aimed at controlling inflation and the deficit. These policies included:

1. Holding government spending below the rate of economic growth in order to break the structural deficit cycle that had been created.

2. Monetarism (manipulation of money supply and interest rates) designed to dampen the economy, restrict the labour market, and break the inflation cycle.

3. Holding wages by imposing wage controls—nominally to break the wage-push inflation cycle but in reality to aid accumulation functions and lower the incidence of strikes.

The wage and price control program, most analysts agree, controlled wages but not prices (Calvert 1984). Some analysts have argued that the controls were aimed specifically at the public sector and quasi-public institutions, such as hospitals (Maslove and Swimmer 1980: 151).

Wage controls succeeded in reducing *real incomes* of workers by just under seven percent (Calvert 1984: 27). As mentioned above, there had been an attempt in the hospital sector to "right a wrong" and narrow the gap with "similar workers in private enterprise" (Isbester 1971: 349). Controls were useful in blocking that movement.

Aside from monetary issues, controls harmed collective bargaining. Some commentators described controls as an attack on human rights "by extinguishing collective bargaining" (Calvert 1984: 33). CUPE began bargaining "as if there were no controls and the AIB did not exist" (Policy Paper, 1975 Convention) in the belief that the controls program did not constitute a legitimate government policy. However, totally ignoring the Anti-Inflation Board was not possible, according to CUPE hospital negotiators who were interviewed. "We refused to negotiate to the guidelines but the hospitals didn't take their eyes off them. Their packages reflected the existence of the AIB," commented one negotiator. The controls, combined with on-going compulsory arbitration, "put the damper on any major gains and really meant losses to us."

The 1975–76 round was the first bargaining under controls. The 1974 bargaining had gone well for the workers. The threat of a strike in Toronto had yielded a $1.50/hour increase and this settlement became the benchmark or standard across the province. This was before wage controls were introduced. The comparison of the bargaining rounds illustrates the effect of controls. Hospital workers had hoped "...to close the gap even more with work outside the hospitals" (Local President, Hamilton). Instead, the government mediator forced them to take the inferior Service Employees International Union (SEIU) settlement which was eventually rolled back by several million dollars. According to Peter Douglas, a staff negotiator, this caused "incredible frustration." The drawn-out process yielded a substandard contract which was significantly rolled back. Many CUPE members wondered if there was any real collective bargaining anymore. As one member put it: "...seems like the Ontario Government mediators should meet with AIB board and hand it [the contract] down." (Member of 1975 CUPE hospital negotiating team, interview, 1985.)

These federal and provincial wage guidelines thus severely altered the collective bargaining process in the hospitals. In any case, this process was already severely distorted from the effects of the *Hospital Labour Disputes Arbitration Act* (HLDAA).

Measures to Weaken Labour's Power: *The Hospital Labour Disputes Arbitration Act*

The Origins

In May of 1963 media editorials were asking whether hospital employees should have the right to strike or whether compulsory arbitration should be imposed. The interest was prompted by a threatened strike at the Toronto General Hospital by the Building Service Employees International Union (BSEIU). The Service Employees also were preparing for strikes at hospitals in Sault St. Marie and Wallaceburg.

Al Hearn, Vice-President of BSEIU and an advocate of compulsory arbitration, admitted that "...the real reason for threatening a strike is to force the Ontario government to look at compulsory arbitration for hospital employees" (*Financial Post*, May 18, 1963, p. 34). Hearn may have been alone in his support for arbitration. Other union leaders wanted the right to strike. Stan Little, President of the National Union of Public Service Employees (and soon to be president of CUPE)[1] claimed any arbitrator appointed by the Government would not be trusted (*Financial Post*, ibid.). He also felt, as did his fellow executive members, that compulsory arbitration would weaken union bargaining power. Unionists feared compulsory arbitration would soon be forced on other sectors of public workers. (Interview, Bill Brown, CUPE Hospital Coordinator, 1980–81, February 1986)

The final incident that created conditions for the provincial government to enact "no-strike" legislation was a three-month conflict at Trenton Memorial Hospital. The Trenton strike, according to Kruger (1985: 55), was used by the government to raise public concern over patient safety during hospital conflicts. This was an old argument but it provided the government with a justification for eliminating the right to strike.

Following the Trenton strike the Province established a three-person Royal Commission to investigate alternatives to strikes in the hospital sector. The board reflected the government's concern with legitimizing any move against the right to strike. The Chairman was Judge C. E. Bennet and his two committee members were R. Hicks, a management consultant, and H. Simon, the Canadian Labour Congress (CLC) Ontario Representative. The Commission recommended legislation that would have given the Cabinet the *discretion* to prevent or to end work stoppages by imposing compulsory arbitration. This discretion was to be applied whenever adequate patient care was threatened or when one party did not bargain in good faith. In the latter case, the other party would have to request arbitration (Kruger 1985: 54).

In 1965, the provincial government ignored its own commission's recommendations, introduced the Hospital Labour Disputes Arbitration Act (HLDAA). The legislation provided for a system of compulsory arbitration prohibiting strikes and lockouts in the hospitals.

---

[1] In 1963 CUPE was formed through the amalgamation of the National Union of Public Employees (NUPE) and the National Union of Public Service Employees (NUPSE). Stan Little was CUPE's first president and held office well into the 1970s.

Years later, the chair of the Ontario Labour Relations Board, George Adams, described why states generally opt for compulsory arbitration and denial of the right to strike in the public sector. Adams cited:

(1) *Protection of sovereignty*: "In simple terms, 'sovereignty' stands for the notion that governments cannot accede to industrial action because to do so would compromise the sovereign authority to govern conferred on the legislative body by the will of the people expressed by the ballot box" (Adams 1981: 225)

(2) *Mitigation of union monopoly*: "The 'monopoly' argument is based on the related notion that most government services are offered on a monopolistic basis causing public sector trade unions to enjoy tremendous (and unfair) bargaining power when they threaten to strike" (Ibid., 226)

(3) *Protection of the public*: "Even assuming that the arguments of sovereignty and monopoly can be overcome, a concern that some or all public employee strikes actually harm the innocent public, or will after a certain duration, remains as a final stumbling block to the wholesale importation of private sector principles to public sector labour relations" (Adams 1981: 227).

These arguments provide a framework within which to view the actions of the provincial government. As we will see below, the reluctance to remove the legislation, in the face of evidence suggesting it should be removed, is linked to the crisis measures of the provincial government. The Government was interested in reducing and controlling union strength.

The Effect of the Hospital Labour Disputes Arbitration Act

CUPE had opposed the introduction of the *Act* and after seven years of operation CUPE formally applied to have it removed. Given CUPE's dominant position in the hospital sector, the union's criticisms of the *Act* held considerable weight. Some of the main ones were:

1. *Arbitrated awards had not narrowed the gap between similar occupations inside and outside of the hospitals.* Government studies such as the Johnson Commission Report [p3. 24–28] verified this.

2. *Settlements were not expedited but seriously delayed.* A 1970 study by the provincial Labour Minister came to similar conclusions (Ontario 1970: 21). Serious implications arise from this, for when a local union is aware that there will be delays and it does not have the right to strike, it takes lower settlements. Negotiators and executives want to get the money to members quickly. A moderately low settlement that takes a long time to come breeds discontent and causes suffering for lower paid workers.

3. *The Act has, to a large degree, destroyed collective bargaining.* CUPE noted there is often indifference to real bargaining: "Employers are often not prepared to make reasonable offers for fear of weakening their position in front of arbitrators. They tend to expect there will be arbitration" (1972, p. 5).

The lower settlements in the hospitals were associated with aspects of the arbitration process, according to CUPE. First, arbitrators seldom know the specific conditions in the hospitals and often are also unaware of the specifics of the bargaining. This leads them to ignore aspects which may affect wage settlements and they simply "cut the difference" between the sides. Second, arbitrators tend to take other *arbitrated* settlements as precedents... "arbitrations influence arbitrations influence arbitrations." The special circumstances of the dispute may be ignored, as was noted in interviews with negotiators and arbitrators (see also CUPE 1972).

The lack of interest in pre-arbitration negotiations has been well researched in Canada. The fear of undercutting positions in front of arbitration boards leads negotiators to withhold compromises. This eliminates the give and take in bargaining. Movements prior to arbitration are often seen as weaknesses in the original demands or at least as a willingness to give even more. The technical names for this phenomenon are the "narcotic effect" and the "chilling effect".

The *narcotic effect* "describes the tendency for parties who have used interest arbitration to rely on it...manifested by choosing arbitration, failing to negotiate a settlement or emulating settlements arbitrated elsewhere" (Gunderson 1983: 28–29). In the hospital sector even CUPE suffers from this to a degree. Several CUPE officers interviewed indicated that, while they would like to get rid of HLDAA, they don't mind using it for nursing homes. This is due to the homes' small staffs and an environment that mitigates against strike. Given the circumstances and the nature of the employer, the arbitration route is easier.

The *chilling effect* refers to the tendency of arbitration to "cool" the bargaining process by encouraging the parties to submit unreasonable offers and discouraging concessions during the negotiating phase. In the extreme, the bargaining process is completely chilled if the parties start far apart on many issues and remain apart throughout negotiations. The chilling effect is alleged to occur in arbitration because the parties act in anticipation of a compromise settlement. The zone of disagreement starts large and stays large because the positions of the parties at the end of negotiation are likely to provide the range within which the arbitrated settlement will be made. The fear that the arbitrator will simply "split the difference" is not the only possible cause of the chilling effect. It may also reflect optimising behaviour if arbitration reduces the uncertainty in the costs of reaching a settlement (Gunderson 1983). (For corroborative comments from the U.S. experience, see Bloom 1981.)

Provincial studies tend to agree with CUPE's assertion that arbitration is negatively affecting bargaining because of the narcotic and chilling effects. The Bales Report (Ontario 1974) found a distinct shift to arbitration since the *Act* was passed and a "distinct decline in the willingness to reach a voluntary settlement" (p. 5).

Another concern about arbitration involves union democracy. Arbitration denies union members full or even major involvement in bargaining. This creates many problems within the unions, often leading to centralization and discontent. Union negotiators may arrive at an agreement with management because it avoids arbitration (which has not been especially successful in the past). What then happens if the membership of the union rejects a memorandum of agreement which the union bargaining team agreed to? There are two possible outcomes. The teams can begin to bargain again and almost assuredly end up in arbitration, or they can go straight to arbitration. Not only does this subvert bargaining but it emasculates the rank and file. *Invariably* an arbitrator will take the original memorandum of agreement as the basis of the arbitrated settlement (Weiler 1981). The union members then get the rejected settlement imposed on them— that is, unless they break the law and strike.

The 1981 arbitration settlement imposed on CUPE had this result. Although CUPE's membership had rejected the memorandum of agreement by a 91% margin, Paul Weiler, in his award, stated he must take the memorandum into account. The "well-negotiated," "voluntary" settlement containing "compromises" could not be dismissed. The arbitrator, like the negotiators themselves "...should treat the [tentative] settlement as fixing the ball park...for the new contract" (Weiler 1981: Section IV). He added: "...the tasks of the interest arbitrator is to try and replicate the results of the process of free collective bargaining. Realistically, this means that a memorandum of agreement must be accepted as definitions of just about the whole range of fringe and contract language" (Section VIII). Weiler himself recognized this contradiction, but the OHA encouraged the arbitrator to use the memorandum of agreement as a basis for the award. CUPE claimed that there was an explicit verbal agreement not to submit the memorandum in arbitration and that this was a condition of signing (Interview, Union Negotiator, February, 1985).

Thus, arbitration can lead to the subversion of the democratic rights of union members. This is further corroborated by the cases, mentioned earlier, where delays in bargaining also push locals to accept inferior settlements, thereby indirectly subverting democracy.

The last difficulty with arbitration concerns the scope of issues that can be dealt with. Issues of pay, vacation or pensions can be measured or counted. The issues of labour process are not so easily evaluated. This reinforces management rights and leaves sources of frustration unresolved.

The perceptions of CUPE members provide interesting corroboration of the criticisms of arbitration raised thus far. A dietary worker of ten years commented:

> There's no...use in it [bargaining]. Might as well walk in and ask "what can we have?" Most people I talk to feel that way. Of course we have to bargain to get anything but if you want the money or any benefits quick you have to back off.

A housekeeper articulates the feeling of not being involved:

> Sure we make our comments about what we want but by the time the negotiators get finished and the government (arbitrator) puts their two cents in we have nothing of what we asked for. I don't go to the meetings anymore—would you?

Some arbitrators have tried different tactics. Kevin Burkett, who arbitrated the 1986 round, sent the two parties back to bargain, telling them to "...pretend it's the 11th hour and there is the right to strike." But as Paul Barry, President of the Ontario Council of Hospital

Unions (OCHU), says, "it's not something one can pretend. If we move and OHA isn't really playing..." (Interview, March, 1986).

The many criticisms made by CUPE, corroboration by government studies, and commentaries by arbitrators all pointed to problems with the industrial relations practices legislated by the provincial government. The Johnston Commission was established to review the these practices and made important proposals based on its investigation.[1] Johnston found: (1) Arbitration had caused noticeable delays in getting settlements (Report: p. 10). (2) The government budgeting process and other actions were influencing the levels of the settlements. (Report: 9, 13, 42).

The settlements reached by arbitration also had several shortcomings, according to Johnston. The hospitals continued to lag behind comparable private sector employment (p. 16–20). Johnston stated: "Employees with no right to strike must be assured equal compensation with others" (p. 22). He further noted that it took the 1974 Toronto hospital workers' strike threat to make a shift in compensation patterns (p. 23). Direct negotiations were also found to be significantly impaired, just as CUPE had charged. Arbitrators were found to be influenced by arbitrators and delays in settlements were acknowledged.

To remedy this, the Johnston Commission proposed that:

1. A uniform province-wide job classification system for hospital employees should be constructed.There should be benchmark positions identified, each with a salary equivalent to a comparable job from outside the hospital.

2. A province-wide bargaining structure should be established for a given set of "central issues" while local negotiations (i.e. at the hospital level) continue for specific issues such as shift scheduling.

3. *Ad hoc* boards of arbitration should be replaced by a permanent panel of chairmen. The parties should be required to conform to dates set by the appointed chairman.

---

[1] All references are from " The Johnston Commission."

4. The Government of Ontario's position as budget setter should be clearly recognized. Given this direct fiscal involvement, the Government should sit at the table as an observer.

It seems likely that the Commission's results did not please key figures in Cabinet. None of the recommendations were acted on. Indeed, in 1979 when the HLDAA was amended, it was simply extended to cover nursing homes and directly-controlled support facilities such as laundries (see Kruger,1985).

The Commission did not look at the right to strike as this was "...outside the guidelines." However, Johnston, in a privately-published article, noted it was unfortunate "...that the pre-HLDAA Act recommendations for limited strike and lockout sanctions were not accepted" (Johnston 1974).

The *Act* was intended to bring stability to the hospitals. It was supposed to eliminate strikes and lockouts. In this respect the *Act* failed. There have been more strikes and threatened strikes in the Ontario hospital sector than in any other provincial jurisdiction except Quebec. Between 1965 and 1972 there were five small walkouts (CUPE, 1972: 2). Between 1972 and 1984 there were three threatened province-wide walkouts and one major confrontation involving 65 hospitals and over 10,000 workers. CUPE puts the blame for these strikes and other actions on the *Act* itself: "...the frustration brought about by the *Act* has caused more strikes in Ontario than in any other province in Canada" (CUPE, 1972: 1).

The *Act* was a major contributing cause of the 1981 strike. It distorted bargaining, helped maintain inequities in salary and conditions of work, and subverted union democracy. Despite evidence suggesting that there were many problems with the legislation, the Provincial Government appears to have left this legislation in place in order to maintain some control over labour's power to oppose changes in working conditions in the hospitals.

3

Women, the Labour Process, and the Strike

The exploration of the role of gender in determining or conditioning collective action is not an easy task. This chapter looks at the gender-specific aspects of the hospital strike. We first discuss the content and meaning of work for women workers. We then move to describe hospital work, reviewing the changes leading to the strike. Finally, we look at the range of issues facing women in unions generally and in CUPE particularly.

The proposition underlying this chapter is this: women were affected adversely by the dramatic changes in the labour process within the hospitals. The changes were taking away some rewards that attracted women to the work in the first place. The dissatisfaction resulted in frustration and eventually militancy because, given the destruction of collective bargaining, there was no other way to deal with the problem. This implies men and women were, *in part*, on strike for different reasons. The public demands of the union were partially the common demands of the members and more probably were the men's total set of demands. The key issues for many of the women were never publicly articulated.

FROM HOME TO HOSPITAL: WOMEN IN SERVICE

Few of us are surprised that over 75% of hospital workers are women. We might be surprised if one said that three-quarters of the steelworkers at Stelco were female. The social acceptance of occupational segregation by sex is entrenched in our society. The acceptance of women as hospital workers comes from the belief that non-professional and semi-professional work in hospitals is "women's work."

Table 3.1: Female Percentage of Selected Industries

	1981
Forestry	24.4
Manufacturing	27.9
Construction	9.4
Transportation and Communication	23.4
Trade	43.3
Finance, Insurance and Real Estate	61.0
Community, Business and Personal Service	60.3

SOURCE: Armstrong and Armstrong, 1984 Table 2, pg. 27.

> The very "feminine" qualities that make women so highly valued in family work explain why they are to be found in such large numbers also in paid work in the service sector. Female skills in relating to other people, in caring for others, in loving, are crucial in both their unpaid family and their paid service work. By socialization, by training, by everyday experience, women are the professionals of servicing (Balbo 1982: 255).

The servicing work that women do in the family is reflected in the jobs done in the labour force. Hospital work, with its food preparation, housekeeping and bedside care, obviously parallels tasks in the home. In many areas of the labour market where women are concentrated, this parallel or resemblance with work in the home is evident. For example, work in a garment factory resembles one kind of work

Table 3.2: Females as a Percentage of Selected Occupations (1981)

Occupation	Female as % of those in the Occupation (1981)
Clerical	98.7%
Medicine (RNA's, Aids and Orderlies)	83.4%
Teaching	63.5%

SOURCE: Armstrong and Armstrong 1984, Table 6, pg. 36.

Table 3.3: Female Labour Force Participation

Year	% Female Participating	Female % of Labour Force
1951	24.0	22.0
1961	29.5	27.3
1971	34.9	34.6
1981	51.8	40.8

SOURCE: Armstrong and Armstrong, 1984, Table 1, pg. 19.

done at home. There is a general gender-based segregation in the labour market.

With the increase in women's participation in out-of-home work, or "paid labour," occupational segregation by sex has not significantly changed. There has been both an industrial segregation of women (i.e. into certain economic sectors) and an occupational segregation (i.e. into certain jobs). The Armstrongs illustrate the extent of industrial segregation:

> In fact the women working in the community, business and personal service sectors represented 43% of *all* women who worked in paid jobs (Armstrong and Armstrong 1984: 27).

While the hospital is not unique, it is a clear example of segregation. The hospital, as part of the health care sector, is generally a female-segregated industry. Within Ontario hospitals occupational segregation is pronounced: 99% of the tradesmen in maintenance are male and 98% of housekeeping and Register Nursing Assistants are female (Torrance 1984: 211–32).

More and more women are entering the work force. Table 3.3 illustrates the increase in participation of women in paid work. The composition of the female work force is shifting to married women. As of 1979 "the female labour force consisted of 30% single, 60% married and 10% other (widowed, separated, divorced) women" (Mackie, 1983: 254). The greatest increase was in married women of childbearing age with pre-school children (Mackie 1983: 254; Fox 1980: 174–75). Traditionally, these have been the women least likely to work in paid jobs. This phenomenon is not uniquely Canadian or North American. Sue Sharpe (1984) found the same trend in Britain.

Why are women, who are mothers of small children, increasingly participating in paid labour? There is a complex of reasons. The key one is necessity. Simply put, women *must* work. Women, as sole income earners or partners in a family, have little choice. Moreover, the need for two incomes has increased, given male salary erosion due to wage controls, inflation, and increased layoffs (Connelly 1978; Fox 1980; Calvert 1981). As Pat and Hugh Armstrong point out:

> Changing economic conditions have been pushing most women into the labour market.... Wages are not keeping pace with prices...making it difficult for women to compensate for their husband's shrinking pay cheques by working harder at home (1983:31).

The Armstrongs refer here to an inabilitiy to make clothes, grow food, or repair things in order to compensate for wage erosion. The household-produced goods of the old days have been made into commodities produced outside the home.

A second pressure that draws women into the work force is the growth of the service sector. This sector attracted and demanded women because it contained many "traditional women's occupations" and it was labour intensive (Mackie, 1986: 255; Armstrong and Armstrong, 1983; Balbo, 1982). The expansion of health and education accounts for a significant part of the demand for women's labour in the service sector. These sectors have expanded quickly and have prompted a concern for restraint, particularly in labour costs (Lalonde 1978; Henderson 1975). The combination of the need for cheap labour, the rapid expansion, and nature of the work made women an excellent choice. Women, in large numbers, had the ability needed and were "in reserve in the home." This means they are "...available for work, cheap and they compete for jobs." (Armstrong and Armstrong 1984: 20–21; Fox 1980; Connelly 1978). Finally, women had the education for these expanding service jobs (Armstrong and Armstrong 1984: 33; see also Lowe, 1980: 361–81).

Besides necessity and the "reserve labour" thesis, women's participation in the paid labour force can be explained by developments that reduced the confining nature of household and parental duties. This was assisted by "...the introduction of more effective contraceptive techniques" that have led to a "decline in the birth rate...which has freed women to enter the paid work force... New technological developments have also been introduced: dishwashers, microwave ovens, washing machines, clothes dryers and vacuum cleaners have

Figure 3.1: General Characteristics of Work for Women

In Home	In Labour Market
Isolation/Individuation	Interaction/Comradery
Partial Intrinsic Reward/No Reward	Extrinsic and Intrinsic Rewards
Invisibility	Formal Recognition

become more common place in Canadian households...decreasing the necessary housework time" (Armstrong and Armstrong 1984: 15).

The motivation of women themselves is another consideration in accounting for the increased labour force participation. Both material and non-material ties bind women to the home. Many men and women previously believed it was not permissible for women to work outside the family. While many still hold that view, there has recently been a shift in attitudes. There is an increase in the acceptability of women working in the paid labour force. Sharpe, in her study of working mothers in England, concluded that women are not only forced to leave the home but many *want* to. The world of home work has changed over the century. The homeworker is more isolated and work at home is viewed as non-productive. It is generally unrecognized, unremunerated, and under-rated. One illustration of this is the reaction of non-homeworkers (generally men) to having to do housework. Studies show that unemployed men who take up housework tasks report feeling downgraded and non-contributory (Yeandle 1984; Sharpe 1984). So, women want to do paid work to regain a measure of reward and identity.

There are also the interrelations between paid and unpaid work to consider. Women seek things in the labour market that they don't get from domestic work. Figure 3.1 outlines some of the common differences between home and labour market work reported by interviewees. Women report that the productive involvement outside the home increases their identity, independence, and power in the family (Sharpe 1984; Pollert 1981: 98). This is seen in our case study as well:

> My husband didn't want me to work but we needed the money. I wasn't sure how things would go when I did start but I like it. I think he takes me more seriously.

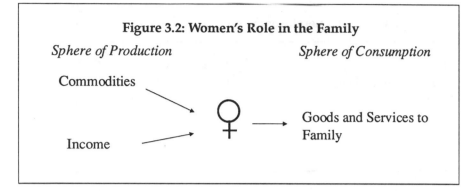

Figure 3.2: Women's Role in the Family

Sphere of Production   *Sphere of Consumption*

Commodities

Goods and Services to
Family

Income

Many female interviewees commented that labour market work is similar in form to work at home. Strictly speaking, this is not true. There are similarities between household work and work outside the home but the rewards and context of the labour differ. The social context and reward system outside the home are, for many, a reasonable trade-off for the illusory freedom of schedule the housewife appears to have. Conceptually, women may be viewed as playing a mediation role, turning resources available to the family into services to fulfill needs, as represented graphically in Figure 3.2. This role places women in a position where they must cope directly with shortfalls in income and general problems facing household maintenance. Women, even as fulltime home workers, have to face the inability to satisfy needs. Women not only mediate resources such as income but deal with the flaws of the system as a whole (Balbo 1982:252). These flaws may include health and safety problems, poor management practices, bankruptcies, layoffs, etc. These flaws can create income shortfalls for the family and frustration, alienation, and health problems for family members. Mediation in this sense is a dual function, involving organizing the resources and ensuring they are converted into a form which permits consumption.

This "mediation" role, with its pressures, makes the positive side of labour market participation even more attractive. Two factors can make paid labour preferable to domestic labour: (1) paid labour increases resources to the woman and her family; and, (2) paid labour in settings such as the hospital brings intrinsic rewards to the service employee and care giver. For the hospital worker, the role of caregiver and participant in the healing process is very important (see Badgely, 1975, for a discussion of non-professionals in healing). As one hospital worker comments:

I like the money sure enough but I also like the guests. I think of 'em like guests that need care. You can sure appreciate how they get better each day. They'd have to pay me a pile more if it weren't for that (Housekeeper, Interview, Hamilton).

In other words, for the hospital worker the rewards are both extrinsic (wage) and intrinsic (personal job satisfaction), and intrinsic job satisfaction is the major part of the complex reward structure that keeps the workers in this work. Changes in that relation to work can upset this delicate balance.

THE CHANGING NATURE OF WOMEN'S WORK IN THE HOSPITAL

In many ways it is safe to say that health care work *is* women's work. In Canada, as of 1971, more than three quarters of hospital staff were female; by 1981, the figure had not dramatically changed (Statistics Canada 2-11 [1971B]). The hospitals were also growth industries, doubling and then tripling in number and staff from the mid-1950s to the 1970s (Torrance 1984; Hospital Statistics, 1977–78: No. 83–232).

Women and Service in the Hospital

This growth industry, which relied on women workers, had been, until 1974, a low-wage ghetto. This ghetto was created as a result of a complex interrelationship between three factors. First, the hospital was an "employer of last resort" and studies show that they employed a high proportion of frail, handicapped, and poorly-educated workers (Torrance 1984). The hospitals also drew from the reserve of women in the home. These two constituencies were used to depress (or justify the depression of) wages. Second, the health service sector's rapid growth and high expansion costs with diminishing revenue returns put demands to cut costs high on the agenda of hospital administrations. Third, hospital work was seen as partially a labour of love, particularly for women (Badgely 1975) and "women are believed to be dedicated to service and not self interest" (Brown 1975: 174).

The wages in the hospitals were so low that some newspapers, such as the *Globe and Mail*, found it scandalous. Wages were "...below what the Economic Council of Canada sets as the poverty line" (*Globe and Mail*, Editorial, April 17, 1969). Moreover, as the fiscal crisis advanced *and* as the economic recession developed, jobs in other sectors

Table 3.4: Characteristics of Work in Major Departments in Hospitals

	Nursing	Housekeeping	Lab	Dietary	Maintenance (Male Dominated)
Primary Job Types for Women	Registered Nursing Assistant; Nursing Aids	Housekeeper; Housekeepers Aid	Lab Tech	Food Preparation; Tray loading, washers	Few Women
Contact with Patient	Yes	Yes	Not Normally	None	Minimal
Care Giving Health or Healing	Yes/bedside	Secondary effects through interaction	Yes/prognosis on tests seen as central to care	Very Minimal	Minimal
Type of Work	Range of care giving	Cleans, disinfects patient surroundings	See above	Special diets for people	Repair and maintain
Level of Job Satisfaction	Rates high	Rates high	Medium-high	Lowest	Not tied to care but to craft work

became very scarce and quitting was a risky proposition. In this context, women hospital workers had to stay where they were. They had to "grin and bear it" or push for change. This constitutes a precondition for collective action—there was no feasible escape from problems at work.

Attachment to Healing

A second condition for collective action revolved around what we termed the "motivation for service work." Women had ties with the care-giving, nurturing, and healing functions of work in the hospital. This surfaced in the interviews. An RNA commented:

> I can't explain the feeling. When someone is heading home, looking better and you know you were part of it. (RNA, Hamilton, 1986)

> Work is work but a lot of the time you get more than money and a sore back—I know that chatting up people helps them—you know we [are] health [care] workers too! (Housekeeper, Hamilton, 1985)

For the women hospital workers this personal attachment was critical in their willingness to take strike action. This attachment to healing is what George Torrance, in his study of a Toronto hospital, called the "core function." He found that the closer people were to the care function of the hospital the greater satisfaction they expressed in their work (Torrance,1978: 21). Those in departments with direct patient contact gained more intrinsic satisfaction from work than those without such contact. Table 3.4 outlines the major "non-profession" work areas and the nature of patient contact and care giving they demand.

George Torrance also found that there was a link between nurturing and women's attitudes to work. There was a distinct "parallel" between home and paid work in nurturing and job satisfaction for women (Torrance 1978: 203). He noted this was not true for men (1978: 203). In each department men had less attachment to work in service to the sick than women.[1]

This was also the case in our study. Most of the men referred to the hospital as a poor place to work. They referred to the pay and aspects

---

[1] For example: 90% of the women in the nursing department expressed the service theme as very important to them while only 48% of the men did so. In housekeeping 44% of women expressed the same primary attachment to providing service while only 11% of the men in the same department did (Torrance 1978).

of the work environment as deterrents to employment. Half of the men did not engage in care giving but most of those that did viewed care giving negatively. Many men felt that service and care giving are used against the workers to get more work or prevent protest. Most men interviewed felt intrinsic rewards were peripheral to their reasons for taking hospital work. Some comments:

> The place can be alright. You make friends, you learn how to make work easier. Sure I like some of the patients but they sure are not the reason I work here. I'm here because I need to feed the wife and kids, buy things for the family—you know... I'm here because this is the best I can get now... I'd work in a place with no patients. It might be better. (Housekeeping, Interview, 1986)

The vast majority of women responded quite differently. The caregiving aspects of work were the "glue" that held them to the job. There were few comments on wages and many on the changes in the labour process.

Since the late 1950s, social scientists who have studied hospitals have noted a loyalty and commitment among the workers to the tasks of the institution. Etzioni (1961) concluded that the hospital had a normative influence as an institution, and it was capable of creating "...a non-utilitarian commitment..." John and Barbara Ehrenreich (1973: 15) found that hospital workers expressed a degree of commitment to service and doing one's best that would be "...beyond the wildest dreams of an industrial personnel manager" (see also Ehrenreich 1978 and Torrance 1976: 16).

In our interviews, we found that the dietary department (sometimes called food services) had the weakest non-utilitarian attitudes. (This is consistent with Torrance's findings.) However, even in this assembly-line atmosphere there were many expressions of the caregiving attachment:

> Some days you lean back and you're so fed up. The speed, the heat, the noise its crazy. A lot of us step back and say to ourselves "someone's eating this." Then a "special" comes by and people are careful—it kind of makes things more worthwhile. (Food assembly line worker, Hamilton, 1986)

The World of Hospital Work

What turned "non-utilitarian" care givers into militant, illegal strikers? An essential consideration was that changes in the labour process broke the normative, care-giving, service link between the women workers and their jobs. Let us look at the nature of work in the various hospital departments and the effects of changes on workers in these departments.

Nursing

The nursing department includes an wide range of work areas, each with its own peculiarity. These are the medical, surgical, and obstetric wards spread throughout the hospital. Typically there are 25–35 beds in groups of four's, two's, and privates. The supervisor is the head nurse and on a day shift one might find several Registered Nurses (RN's), three or four Registered Nursing Assistants (RNA's) and possibly a ward clerk. Orderlies and porters, the male jobs, are now centrally dispatched on request.

Patients differ widely. Some are very ill or bedridden on post-operative recovery. Others are in for tests and feel healthy and energetic. These differences affect the type of work that must be done.

Typically RN's and RNA's attend rounds (a report of the patient's condition) at the start of a day shift. The RNA is assigned a number of patients for care. The cycle of medication, food, vital signs, cleaning, testing, etc. begins and runs throughout the shift.

Special "prepping" is done for those going to surgery. For others, there is a range of care, such as dressing changes, administering special injections, etc. The RNA is only allowed to do certain procedures. Nurses are required for many functions, e.g. blood samples or intravenous work.

The RNA's work usually includes bedside care, such as back rubs, dressing changes, bedpans and enemas. Their contact with patients used to be intense and continuous. When the nurse does the bedside work, or it goes undone, frustration for the RNA is the result.

In the 1970s, the measures outlined in Chapter 2 began to affect the RNA's. There was a restriction of bedside care. Patients and family members had to do some of the bedside work. As well, many hospital administrations began replacing RNA's with RN's, although not on a one-to-one ratio. Fewer RN's were employed full-time. There were two reasons for this. First, the RN's were easier to hire on a part-time basis. This meant hospitals could use an RN for peak times, such as early morning to handle meals, then let her go. Second, the hospitals shortened patient stays (or turn-around time) so the level of acute care needed, on average, increased. Hospitals were also shifting some of the recovery time from the hospital to the home while cutting back on labour—the average patient who previously stayed five to twelve days in the hospital now stayed only three to five days (Stoddard 1984). According to management, the RN was better trained for this increased acute care. CUPE has resisted this move by arguing: (1) there is no evidence RNA's cannot handle the increased responsibility; and, (2) the best way to deliver health care in the hospital is through a team approach, including both RN's and RNA's; and, (3) hiring fewer persons to cover the displaced RNA's lowers the standards of health care and, if the same number of RN's were hired to replace the lower paid RNA's, the cost would be prohibitive (White 1987).

Losing RNA's, dealing with sicker patients, and severely cutting back on bedside care took a toll on the staff. RNA's were angry and upset.

> The world was becoming backward. Budgets and timetables meant more than patients. (RNA, Hamilton)

> I know I wasn't alone in feeling hurt, our jobs were downgraded and health care was hurt. (RNA, Hamilton)

> By 1981 I had ten last straws. I was either going to quit or strike. (RNA, Burlington)

Kitchens (Dietary; Food Services)

In contrast to other areas of the hospital, kitchens have the most direct supervision and the most factory-like conditions. Patient meals are generally loaded on a conveyor belt system. Food aides (or dietary aids) load up the stations (juice in glasses, for example), then the trays move past the stations and workers put on the appropriate foods and implements. The belt moves quickly and workers must move quickly too. After the trays are loaded, delivered, and returned, they are cleaned. Trays are stripped and plates scraped and put into sterilizing washers. Pots, juice containers, and the like have to be scrubbed.

The dietary workers expressed a more traditional attitude to the workplace. This is not surprising given that their working conditions and the management style were more similar to a manufacturing unit. The push to cut costs in the late 1970s meant speeding up the pace of work. Workers resented both the increased supervision and the speed ups. Some senior workers recalled times past when there was consultation about special diet trays. They recalled how food service workers had gone out to deliver trays to get comments and suggestions on how they could improve service and quality. This closer contact with care giving had created a better attitude to work.

The food services areas generally have a much higher proportion of male workers than is the case for nursing. As with most males interviewed, the care aspect of work was secondary to such issues as protecting the sick leave plan and other monetary considerations. Women, on the other hand, expressed a desire to restore the work back to what it had been—reduce the speed and increase the patient contact. *This is in line with our observation that different attitudes were evident between men and women.*

Housekeeping

This department is a microcosm of changes in the hospital generally. The work world of those in housekeeping has changed a great deal in the last 15 years. In the years preceding the strike, the housekeeping department had both male (cleaners) and female (housekeepers or maids) workers. The men would mop the floors, sweep, do a range of polishing jobs and dispose of garbage. The men were considered to have easier work routines than the women but they had two wards to cover. This meant less patient contact and socializing for the men (see Torrance 1978: 173–75). Males were somewhat pushed out of the department in the 1970s and early 1980s, and the "cleaner" classification in many hospitals was partially, or completely, phased out.

Women looked after the rooms. This involved dusting and cleaning both rooms and bathrooms. Sometimes this included changing flower water, etc. If a patient was discharged, the routine varied. It was necessary to sterilize (i.e. carbolize and put fresh linen on the bed). Night tables and other immediate fixtures would also have to be sterilized. This was a heavy, time-consuming job.

In the early 1970s the housekeeper had "her ward." She knew the nurses, had regular contact with patients and the pace or routine was reasonable yet varied depending on the rhythm of discharges. Housekeepers helped set the atmosphere and thereby contributed to the patient's recovery. The housekeepers interviewed typically report:

> I've made some real friends over the years. A good head nurse doesn't bother you if you stay with someone and have a wee talk. The dears [patients] appreciate it…the days are better for them—I must say I liked it too. (Housekeeper of 17 years, Hamilton, Interview)

> Some of the younger girls say "why spend your time chatting up all the patients?" I tell them that if the most exciting thing that happens in the day is rolling over then you need some talk. You almost be a mother I guess—and it does wonders. (Housekeeper of 13 years, Hamilton, Interview)

The seventies brought further changes. The patient stays were shortened and housekeepers' work changed in several ways. First, the pace increased because housekeepers had to do the heavy and time-consuming carbolizing and linen change. Second, the atmosphere altered. Patients, on average, needed more acute care and therefore were less responsive. This meant that employee-patient bonds were more difficult to establish. The woman housekeeper was more isolated. Cleaning at the hospital became more similar to cleaning at home. Some housekeepers refer obliquely to this:

> Some days I think, oh baby, lets just stay home but I knows cleaning here and cleaning at work is all the same. (Housekeeper, Hamilton)

Lastly, the housekeeper could no longer play a role in the recovery process, nor see the effect of the health care patients were getting. The patients were gone before housekeepers could see the final recovery stage. This eliminated the stage when patients were eager to talk and looked well. The housekeeper had lost the tie to care giving.

In addition to patient stay, the location of work was altered. Previously a housekeeper's ward was something

> ...you could point to and say—this is mine, I do the work. You know—pride. (Housekeeper, Hamilton)

The hospitals started giving housekeepers multiple wards, moving them around every few days and increasing the pace of work to improve productivity. The transfer of some aspects of the male job to women also increased the workload. These changes, and the more "management" style of supervision, frustrated the housekeepers and reduced their pride in the work.

> We got frustrated—couldn't do it all or do it well. You end up sticking your name on something saying it's done when it isn't.

Housekeepers felt manipulated:

> They played on our feelings, "protect the patient" you get this "do you want germs to spread" or "don't you care how they [patients] feel," to try and get more work—but they were letting everything go to hell! (Housekeeper, Hamilton)

The housekeepers, like the RNA's, saw in a change in their own work and in the process of hospital delivered health care:

The patient use to be king...now they are mass produced. The care is really gone down. (Housekeeper, Hamilton)

Sure housekeeping had deteriorated, everything had deteriorated. Some days it nearly drove me to tears. (Housekeeper, Hamilton)

A system of calling in temporaries for heavy periods, increasing part-time workers and cutting back full-time staff further aggravated the situation.[1]

There is a problem with floats. After you get over not having the full time Mary or whoever around you still have other problems. Floats can't take, you know like pride in the work. They are only in a ward for a day or two then off to a different place. (Housekeeper, Burlington)

The changes in management style meant that old systems of dialogue and problem solving were eliminated.

We use to know our administrators and we had our old style ways of solving problems. That went out the window with all the changes. (Housekeeper, Hamilton)

To summarize, for the housekeeper the labour process was substantially changed. The patient-worker bond was broken, the rewards for the housekeeper consisting of their pride and satisfaction were reduced, and traditional pathways to problem solving were closed. Our conclusion is based on Hamilton and area interviewing only; however, the research department of CUPE and Paul Barry, the Ontario leader of the hospital workers, verify that these types of changes were taking place across the province.

The Laboratories

The labs are not always organized into the prevailing service union at the hospitals. In the Hamilton hospitals we studied, laboratory technologists (lab techs) were in CUPE and played a role in the strike. The labs are a complex place to describe because of the different tests they run and the hardware they use. We will look only at the per-

---

[1] Part-time workers are not always members of the CUPE bargaining unit at the hospitals studied. They, therefore, did not take part in the collective action. For this reason part-time workers were excluded from this study. Anyone interested should look at Pat and Hugh Armstrong's two articles," More For the Money" (1986) and "Female Complaints" (1986) for an analysis of part-time work in the hospitals.

ceived changes in the work and the reactions of the laboratory technicians to these changes.

In the period under study, laboratory technicians reported an increase in demands for productivity:

> The number of tests that come in has gone up about three times...we can't handle it—people ask what am I doing here. (Laboratory Technician, Hamilton)

The rhetorical question was easily answered by laboratory technicians who, without exception, commented that they *felt* the link between their work and patient health and safety.

> I feel under constant pressure—have to be right—someone's dying upstairs. Sometimes I can't be sure. I move so fast."

Another says:

> When I started here the place was spotless and the pace not bad. You had a chance to check your work—not now, it's filthy and it's go, go, go till you're gone."

And a last comment:

> You feel guilty, I know the RNA's are the same—you are there for the patient but the job you do has to be crap sometimes."

The shorter patient stays, with their higher proportion of acute care cases, and the general increase in test requests (due to malpractice fears) pushed up the workload. The way the tests "come in" has also changed:

> Maybe 10 or 20% of the tests used to be stat (emergency) now they label nearly everyone that way, it means nothing."

Supervision has also changed in the labs. The higher paid laboratory technicians have come under closer scrutiny by personnel departments and pressure for increasing test processing rates is common.

The workers also reported less time is spent consulting in the labs now. Although one can still talk over medical questions, one can no longer talk over management questions. This has led to the closing of traditional pathways for problem solving.

Reactions to Change

The changes in the labour process, both in work and management style, had seriously affected the women working in the hospitals. The heavier work and faster pace were important irritants, but the crucial changes revolved around the women's relationship to the *delivery of health care to people*. This is the service aspect to which women were attached. The changes mentioned above broke women hospital workers away from patients. Whether it was RNA's pulled from the bedside or housekeepers moved from ward to ward, the effect was similar. There was frustration with the lack of participation in health care and anger over the deterioration of health care. More than three-quarters of those interviewed made unsolicited criticisms of the declining quality of service. An RNA put it this way:

> It was bad enough that RN's were replacing us but for me to be pushed out of many bedside care duties—it was degrading...I'm not the only one who felt hurt and the care given was hurt too. (RNA, Hamilton)

The bond with care-giving work had been damaged and there would inevitably be a reaction. What was it to be? The options were narrowing. The old informal system where workers talked with supervisors and middle management had been eroded. The union provided the only other mechanism for responding and it had been a useful one in many ways but the hospital workers had poor experiences in the past with the negotiation process. As we saw in Chapter 2, wage controls, no right to strike, and compulsory arbitration severely hampered negotiations. Women commented that:

> Sure we make our comments about what we want but by the time the negotiators get finished and the government [arbitrator] puts their two cents in we have nothing of what we asked for. (Housekeeper)

The problems in the formal process of negotiation in the hospital sector effectively closed this other "traditional" pathway to problem solving. This angered women hospital workers and pushed them to consider options such as a strike.

At many points throughout the events leading to the strike, senior- and middle-level union staff and elected officers tried to dissuade union members from striking. For example, Pat O'Keeffe, CUPE Regional Staff Director, said:

> I told them straight out. You cannot win this—you shouldn't go. They would not listen to me.

Why did these "passive" women go against the advice and instruction of their union? Part of the answer to this question lies in the relationship between women and unions and how this affected their participation in collective action.

WOMEN IN UNIONS; WOMEN ON STRIKE

There is a deep-rooted conviction in our society that women are passive, non-competitive, and acquiescent (Purcell 1979; Pollert 1981; Mackie 1984). Many interviewees in this study said that the strike occurred *despite* the large number of women workers. This view parallels the "popular explanation" of the strike (see Chapter 1). The women members *had* to be led (or misled) by a small group of agitators. Viewing women as non-combative makes it possible to interpret the decision to strike not as a conscious choice made by workers but as an aberration. The aberration can be explained by ignoring the causes that would lead women to strike and looking for external causes. Then the strike becomes a created event with little foundation and women become pawns. Roy McMurtry, the then Attorney General, captured this thinking in his public statement sending hospital workers back to work: "...participants are being swept away by leaders...do not be misled by union leaders whose priorities...are not yours" (McMurtry 1981).

Despite the overwhelming opposition to their strike actions by the government, hospital authorities and their own union leaders, women hospital workers overwhelmingly voted to strike and carried it out. To explain this we must look at the place women hold in the union and the relationship between unions, the paid workplace and home.

General Views On Women and Unions

Little was written on the relationship between women and unions before the late 1970s. The earliest Canadian studies tend to be quite negative in their assessment of the benefits of unions for women. Marchak (1977: 209) concludes in her study that unions are not helpful to white-collar women. She suggests women should create their own unions to improve their working conditions (see White 1980: 53–58). This echoes the analysis by Jean Rands in *Women Unite* where the continuing division of labour along gender lines is attributed to male-dominated unions. A study done in New Brunswick by Joan MacFarland comes to similar conclusions. MacFarland (1979: 47–48) concluded that unions are usually of no benefit and may even be a hindrance to women.

Such views are extreme but they highlight the fact that there are problems faced by women in the unions. Julie White's 1980 study, *Women and Unions*, examines women in unions and challenges the above-mentioned studies. MacFarland, White points out, "...has made no comparison with the situation of non-unionized women, only a comparison to an unspecified standard of her own..." (White 1980: 53–54). This is not sufficient, in White's opinion, to draw conclusions on the utility of joining a union.

This criticism of MacFarland is the main one, but not the only one. MacFarland's study could also be criticized on the grounds that: (1) the mix of groups she studied bears no resemblance to any pattern of women's employment; (2) there is an over-emphasis on small (under 50 employee) shops which are often difficult for unions to organize, regardless of gender composition; (3) the scale created to compare contracts is not based on any consistent criteria and comments such as "uninspired" or "pernicious" reveal the biases of the author; (4) MacFarland's conclusions are not based on comparative data; (5) MacFarland makes unsubstantiated and erroneous comments (for example, she states that in those unions where women are a minority, they can win higher pay, improved working conditions and fringe benefits, but will not make gains on part-time status or maternity leave "through the union channel.")

The criticisms of Marchak's study are more complicated. White argues that Marchak uses a biased *employer-determined* interview sample (White 1980: 58). This, concludes White, leads to a sample of non-unionized workers that would be "...artificially biased towards those with competitive pay rates. It would then appear unionization did not benefit worker's pay rates" (ibid.). A second major problem, according to White, is the limited sample. With 307 respondents and the multiple cells that she must create, the data do not allow one to draw the conclusions she did (White 1980: 57). White's criticisms are reasonable, particularly with respect to the biased sample. This, in itself, is enough to give Marchak's conclusions a shaky foundation. A second problem is Marchak's underestimation of the advantages that are accrued to capital through the maintenance of lower wages for women. She can be interpretted as placing too much responsibility for these lower female wages on the male unionists and their "male unions" based on male fears of competition. Marchak has subsequently acknowledged this and reversed her position (Marchak 1987).

Subsequent studies have come to different conclusions than MacFarland. Julie White's (1980) study is representative of most investigations. After examining pay, fringe benefits and rights issues, she concludes women who belong to unions usually have more protec tion and benefits than those who are non-unionized. This conclusion is reached notwithstanding the continuing and serious problems facing women, both at work and within their unions. Similarly, Pat and Hugh Armstrong, on the basis of their study, comment:

> Unions are a long way from providing female workers with complete protection for a number of reasons: only a minority of women belong; women's concerns, especially over part-time work, have not been a priority in many unions; and unions are seldom as powerful as the employers they face. But their rapidly growing union membership indicates that, contrary to rumour, most women are not opposed to collective action. Women in unions have at least some protection, and almost all female workers are better off organized...While many of the women who are unionized are dissatisfied with some aspects of their union, virtually all are convinced there are significant advantages to being organized. (1983: 110, 119)

Cuneo (1986) also stresses the achievement *women* have made within unions, in part, against a tide of patriarchal employer action and patriarchal unionist action and thinking. Briskin (1983) also emphasizes the achievements by women members in the union movement. She notes:

> In the last ten years, women's activity in unions has had a tremendous impact: policies have been passed, education programs undertaken, progressive demands for women have been brought to the bargaining table. But in spite of a few important breakthroughs...the situation that women face in the work force has not improved significantly....we recognize the potential of using unions to address women's concerns. Although we are, in this sense, prounion, we do not idealize the current structures and policies of the union movement...We know that to make significant gains for women in the workplace unions must be restructured. (1983: 270–71)

Thus, it seems that while women and women's issues have not been a priority in the unions, and have even been subverted in the past, the late 1970s and early 1980s saw a slow and continuous improvement.

There have also been some minor studies of CUPE. The first study of women in CUPE came about as a result of the 1970 Royal Commission on the Status of Women. Grace Hartman, then Secretary-Treasurer of CUPE, argued that if CUPE was to press for implementation of the recommendations of the Commission in the wider Canadian society, the union itself would have to change. The change should involve acting on the Commission recommendations that applied to CUPE. (See CUPE 1971: 3.)

The Status of Women in CUPE described several key problems facing women:

(1) Women are under-represented in proportion to their numbers at every level of CUPE. Only 2 of 17 National Executive board members were women and only 10% of delegates to the 1969 Convention were women. More than one-half of the 149 locals with majority women members had male presidents and only one staff representative in Canada was a woman.

(2) There was a widespread belief among male unionists that women are only secondarily workers and should be at home. This provides a basis for discriminatory actions by unions.

(3) Pay inequities between men and women for similar work exist and non-gender-biased job evaluations are necessary to correct this.

(4) Wage discrimination exists between nursing assistants and orderlies and this reflects sexual discrimination.

(5) Job designations exist where some jobs are labelled female, others male.

(6) A number of clauses in CUPE contracts are clearly discriminatory to women. These include lesser pensions, employment conditions based on marital status, inadequate maternity leave, part-time provisions and lack of daycare. (CUPE 1971: 7–35)

Seven years after this pamphlet was issued, Giroux (1978) did one of the few CUPE contract studies on clauses affecting women. She compared several public sector unions with CUPE and found few substantial differences among the unions (1978: 147). In reviewing CUPE hospital contracts she found many weaknesses. These included:

(1) No seniority accumulated during maternity leave.

(2) No paid maternity from employer.

(3) No adoption leave.

(4) No leave of absence for family illness.

(5) No leave *with pay* for union work.

(6) Some jobs were designated by gender.

(7) No adequate part-time worker's provisions.

(8) No sexual harassment protection.

(9) Life insurance and pension provisions discriminated against women.[1]

The data do not allow us to state whether CUPE fares better or worse than other unions. CUPE is well known for its written and public statements on the need to push for women's equality at work and in the unions. The extent to which this has been achieved would require a major study. While CUPE was aware of problems in women's elected representation, union participation, and contract protection, as of 1981 it had not solved them. The causes of these "problems" are important, but before we move on to these we shall examine some trends for women in unions and in CUPE.

Women's Unionization, Participation, and Representation in Unions

The Unionization of Women

The 1970s was a decade of rapid unionization of women. Table 3.5 shows an increase in the absolute number of women unionists and an increase in the number of women as a percentage of all union mem-

---

[1] The importance of these clauses to women may not be self-evident. Contract language allows enforcement of rights in the workplace. It assists workers in pushing their thinking toward greater reform. It encourages women unionists to participate as it gives confidence and encourages more pro-union thinking.

The importance of the clauses chosen by Giroux varies:

Seniority issues: Seniority is an expression of the credit given for service. It is assumed in the idea of seniority that as one works longer, one's abilities and worth as an employee increases. Women are penalized for childcare and child bearing in this system because they don't accumulate seniority when off for extended maternity leave. In many cases women lose all their seniority when they take leave. This implies women will get fewer promotions, be unable to compete for jobs and get lower wages.

Maternity issues: Women have been treated as solely responsible for child bearing and child rearing. Despite our lip service to the importance of this task, we penalize women in wages, promotions and union involvement. This is closely linked to other issues such as seniority.

Hours of work: Women have been primarily responsible for childcare and housework. This means things like compulsory overtime have a disastrous effect on schedules. The positive advantages of flex time, family sickness leave or voluntary compressed work weeks are many for a person organizing a "double day."

Table 3.5: The Number of Women in Unions Over Time

Year	Number of women members	Percentage of all members
1962	248,884	16.4
1963	260,567	16.6
1964	276,246	16.7
1965	292,056	16.6
1966	322,980	17.0
1967	407,181	19.8
1968	438,543	20.4
1969	469,235	21.2
1970	513,203	22.6
1971	558,138	23.5
1972	575,584	24.2
1973	635,861	24.6
1974	676,939	25.2
1975	711,102	26.0
1976	750,637	27.0
1977	782,282	27.7
1978	835,263	28.7
1979	890,365	29.3
1980	932,883	30.2
1981	979,862	31.0
1982	985,376	32.3

SOURCE: C.A.L.U.R.A., Part II, 1983, Table 24, p. 45.

bers. The number of women unionists rose by 81.7% between 1970 and 1980. This continued a trend that began in the 1960s (CALURA 1982). The increase has continued since 1980.

The rise in absolute numbers paralleled an increase in the proportion of union members who were female. Table 3.5 shows that the distribution of union members by sex shifted substantially. Women were unionizing faster than men. However, as Cuneo (1986) cautions, women remained under-represented in the trade union movement:

> By 1982, for example, only one quarter or 25% of women non-agricultural paid workers in the labour force were unionized; in contrast, 38.2% of the male non-agricultural paid workers were unionized.

The explanation for this pattern of unionization is complicated. The under-representation of women in unions is often attributed to chauvinist attitudes on the part of unions or anti-union feelings among women (White 1980: 50; Briskin 1983: 13). There can be little doubt that these are partial explanations. But three important structural factors also play a role. First, historically, unionization drives often began in work areas where women were not employed. This was a result of the general division of labour based on gender but it also reflects a chauvinism on the part of the union organizations. Second, it was not until the 1960s that women began entering the labour market in large numbers (if we ignore the war years). Third, traditionally unions have usually avoided recruiting drives in small units for a variety of reasons—including time, difficulty, and expense. White (1980: 51) notes that women workers are concentrated in smaller shops. Also, the sectors where women are concentrated have often encountered determined employer opposition to union drives. The banks, retail (e.g. Eatons), and personnel services are examples (White 1980: 50).

The large influx of women into unions is partially explained by the large influx of women into paid labour and the removal of constraints on public sector organizing. In the late 1960s and throughout the 1970s, the public sector was unionized at a remarkable rate. This was due to a change in the legal framework that permitted unionization, a policy of encouraging unions in some jurisdictions, and the rapid growth of the public sector in general. The predominance of women in this sector ensured a rapid growth in women's unionization. A final consideration was the unions' own interest in organizing: unions were spurred on to organize by the huge slump in members due to shutdowns and layoffs in the recession. The "interest" in keeping memberships up paralleled the drop in male members (see Cuneo 1986b).

Women's Participation in Unions

The increase in the number of women union members in the 1970s should have produced an increased participation of women in union affairs. One measure of influence and participation is the percentage of elected officials who are women (see White 1980; Briskin 1983a; Giroux 1978). For the union movement as a whole, there is dramatic under-representation of women. In 1975, women represented 26% of all union members, yet they held only 9% of the senior executive

Table 3.6: Selected Executive Board Members (EBM's)
for Unions in Canada

	1975	1980
All Unions EBMs	1166	944
Women EBMs	116	160
% of Total	**9.0**	**17.0**
National Unions EBMs	541	578
Women EBMs	74	126
% of Total	13.7	21.8
CUPE EBMs	**17**	**17**
Women EBMs	2	4
% of Total	**11.7**	**23.5**
Hospital Locals	*1978*	*1986*
Total Presidents	50	69
Women Presidents	23	44
% of Total	**46.0**	**64.0**

SOURCE: Briskin 1983 (All Unions Data and National Unions); CUPE Research Department Documents (CUPE Data); Archival Materials, Minutes, Bargaining Documents (Hospital Locals).

---

positions. By 1980, women represented 30.2% of unionists but had only 17% of the executive positions. Despite the slight relative increase in executive members, there was still a serious under-representation of women in union leadership positions.

CUPE fared well above the average, but since more than 40% of the CUPE membership are women, the extent of the under-representation is clear. Table 3.6 shows that the hospital unions in the pre-strike (pre-1981) period had a better than average representation of women in executive positions, but here again women represent close to 70% of the members.

Deterrents to Women's Participation in Unions

If the numbers of women unionists *are* increasing, why are women so under-represented as leaders of union activities? A popular explanation is that women participate in union affairs to a lesser extent than men. This is a circular argument. The same conditions that create blocks to women becoming leaders also affect their involvement in union affairs. A number of interrelated factors seem to account for women's lack of involvement in unions. These can be broken down into several categories: (1) time and the relation between home work and an outside job; (2) union activities (what the union actually does) and, (3) union structure (or *how* the union organizes its work) . One can gain insights into women's participation and representation in the unions if we examine these in greater detail.

Time: When to do Union Work?

To determine why women are under-represented and have reduced union participation, we can first look at the homework/outside work relationship. This question of time can be examined in several ways because it has many dimensions. The most common way to look at time constraints is quantitatively, and in this context we acknowledge the concept of the "double" or "triple day."

Women, as noted earlier, have remained primarily responsible for the organization of the household. Society continues to expect women to provide the basis of social reproduction. Women are also expected to provide a range of emotional/educational/psychological services. This has been so, even as women's labour force participation mounts. Studies repeatedly show that the increase in the time that husbands contribute to housework, when both adults work, remains minimal (Yeandle 1984; Gannage 1986; Mackie 1983; Meissner 1977).

Women find themselves having to work all day, then having to go home and do the most of the work at home. To be able, on top of this double day, to take on union responsibilities, such as going to meetings, preparing grievances or whatever, is to accept a triple day.

> While the men had time to go to union meetings after work women had to rush home to their children and to prepare meals. The double day of labour was the most important factor that made it difficult for women to participate actively in their union. (Gannage 1986: 175)

For those women who accept this triple day, union work replaces or becomes their leisure time.

And then I have union work on top of it, so... But I've always worked so I've learned to adjust...I suppose you just look at your priorities in life. I have to have time for my job; I have to have time for my family and I have to have time for me. And the time for me is union work. That's what I'd like to do, that is what I want to do and that is what I enjoy doing. And so the time I set aside for me is always for the union. (Armstrong 1983: 203)

Susan Yeandle noted a similar trend in her British study. One of her interviewees echoes a common refrain "...and you need to be so dedicated, you know, in a thing like that [union]. You've got to be prepared to put a lot of your own social life into it" (Yeandle 1984: 116). In our study, the comments were similar. A clerical worker noted:

I was going to quit the union—not because I was angry but I needed time to have some social life. I thought I'd never get married if I didn't.

A laboratory technologist:

I took a break [from union work] for a while. With a new marriage and home I had real problems—you know what I mean.

A dietary worker in her forties puts it bluntly:

My only leisure time is "Gotum" time—that's "goin to union meetins."

Time has many meanings and it is, in part, socially constructed. It is not simply the number of hours. Time is related to the quality of life, the range of commitments, personal relations, the individual, etc. In some cases it is quantitative, such as how to do many things in a short time. In other cases it is qualitative, such as how to spend quality time with one's children or spouse. At other times it is personal, where one needs the stress release of flexibility. In all cases it is conditioned by the gender relations in society (amongst other important factors). For women there are many faces to "gender time" and we identify three in relation to our study.

(i) Men have women, women have themselves

Study after study shows similar marriage patterns amongst unionists. Pat and Hugh Armstrong (1983), Gannage (1986) and White (1980) all find that active male unionists tend to be married, between 24 and 40, with children. Active women unionists tend to be unmarried, older, with no children at home. Nancy Guberman's study (1983: 276) of the Confederation of National Trade Unions (C.N.T.U.) in Quebec probably best sums up the trend.

More than half of the women in the CNTU study do not have children. As the demands of militancy increase in the upper echelons of
the hierarchy, the number of women with children significantly de-
creases. The opposite is true of men. All of the women in the study
agreed that children and a family are major obstacles to participation in union activities. When we asked members "Do your children
limit your involvement in your union?," 81.8% of the women and
only 33.3% of the men said yes.

Gannage (1986: 179) points out that men could go off to the union
meetings or events and know that food will be cooked, kids will be
taken care of, and all would be watched. Women, on the other hand,
did not have this luxury. Aside from finding another woman, a
friend, or hired stranger, their options were closed.

This interaction between home and paid work is one aspect of the
general deterrent to union activity for women. Men depend on
women to create the time for them to be union activists; women, on
the other hand, must rely on their own initiatives and work if they are
to be activists. The desire to have a family and a stable home environment is a dilemma for women who wish to participate in union affairs.

(ii) No time to get ahead

Many active trade unionists look at the disproportionate numbers
of men and women in leadership positions differently than does the
dispassionate researcher. Union activists know that to get into elected
positions, one has to have "paid one's dues." This means working in
the organization for extended periods in different capacities. In the
unions there is a type of "seniority system" just as there is in the
workplaces. Women, for reasons already mentioned, "lose" their
union seniority or build it more slowly because of the demands of the
home and the workplace. The service breaks taken for maternity pull
women out of union activities. This absence is not a "tolerated" or
"unpunished" phenomenon. A woman returning to union work may
not start where she left off before the leave. In the unions, with cau-
cusing and "political machines," the reintegration into the political
process is even more difficult. Activist women find pregnancy hurts
or removes chances for leadership. Jane Stinson (1978) makes a similar analysis. She extends the point to explain why women are found
in local level leadership positions where there is a demand for a great
deal of work but are not in senior union positions (see also White

1980: 66–67). A lower level of "union seniority" is needed to hold positions at the local level.

Another aspect is the timing of meetings. Holding meetings, conventions, workshops, and educational sessions after hours or on weekends creates difficulties (see White 1980; Gannage 1986; Stinson 1978). Women find it difficult to attend all the functions and do the mingling, discussing, arguing and general participating necessary to gain election. This penalty for maternity and other breaks in participation is a second form of the time constraint for women (see also Hartman 1976).

(iii) Tension and guilt

> "Do you know how a five year old can make you feel about being away, not to mention your husband?"

This housekeeper from a Hamilton hospital puts her finger on a third problem facing women unionists. Guilt and pressure come from the family when "Mom" is out of the house after "work hours." Union women who are activists often report pressure from husbands wishing them to limit union activities, even if "home work" is "getting done" (see Purcell 1979: 128–29). One of Yeandle's interviewees (1984: 116) makes a common comment, "I'm just an ordinary member now. Because I found it too much, at home really a lot of pressure was put on me..."

The key here is not so much that physical aspects of housecleaning or food preparation don't get done. The reasons lie more in the other service roles expected of women in the home in a patriarchal family system. The woman in a traditional home is expected to be there if the male or the children need comforting, advice, or organization. She is supposed to be available for sexual relations. As the Pat and Hugh Armstrong point out in *The Double Ghetto* (1984), women are held responsible for household management, tension management, and sexual relations in a marriage (see also Luxton 1980).

These responsibilities are non-stop. The availability for service or "on call" demands of the women in a family is affected by union activity. This leads to pressure on the women activist and guilt.

> I really had my eyes on doing something in the union you know cleaning things up, make it run better. People told me I could do a good job. I wanted to be more than a steward. My husband says I can go back to the union. I know he doesn't really mean he wants me to. I've been away five years though—I wonder if I know the people? (Laboratory Technician, Hamilton Hospital)

This is not to support that women would be willing to spend each waking moment on union work except for the pressure placed on them by husbands and children. The time constraints placed on women unionists in many ways only reflect the manner in which, among other things, the relation between home and paid workplace is organized in our society.

An interesting question arises when we consider the problem of time in relation to the 1981 strike. Why did the time constraints not block women's participation in the strike? There were few reports of spouses either encouraging their partner to strike-break or not to be active in the strike. A more common response to the strike was for husbands to accept more responsibilities in the home so that their spouses could participate. Family members, friends, and other union members also provided support which permitted women's involvement. This may be related to the level of commitment of the women involved in the strike, which itself is related to the meaning of the work for these women workers.

Action: What the Union Does

In 1976 Grace Hartman, former National President of the Canadian Union of Public Employees, said that one reason women are not actively involved in unions was misinformation. She claimed schools and some media portray unions as "foreign-run, gangster-type operations." A woman's image of unions "...is one of strikes, violence and corruption" (1976: 246). When interviewed in 1986, she reiterated this view. Hartman added that for an average member the union's actions seem (and are) "above board." The actual behaviour, in and of itself, of the union is important. "It is not only a question of seeming democratic and reasonable but of taking up issues of concern to your members" (Hartman, interview, 1986).

The many deterrents to union participation will not be overcome if a union's activities do not serve purposes women identify as important. Women and men have different interests depending on many things, such as family circumstances, job classification and years of service. Despite divergent opinions, there must be a perceptible thrust in union activity aimed at serving the needs of women members. This becomes even more important because of the time constraints on women. Often women cannot take part in the social aspects of union involvement. The comradery, after-meeting beer, chats, and general socializing are not possible for many women due to the constraints outlined above. This means that collectivism and social ties do not keep women in the movement as much as men. It also means that, in this context, the unions are bastions of male culture. The actual achievements of the union in areas important to women, or at least the clear attempt to make these improvements, is even more relevant given the "social isolation." If the union is taking up issues of importance to the female members, women may try to overcome the time-related obstacles and get involved.

Many social scientists (Marchak 1975; MacFarland 1978; Briskin 1983b; Gannage 1986) report that unions often put the declared women's issues low on their priority list and tend to substitute traditional demands around wages. The issues that have been put lower on the list include, for example: pay equity, daycare, and extended maternity leave benefits. CUPE's 1971 assessment of its own policies toward women showed some serious problems in this regard. CUPE charged itself with treating women as second-class members in some locals, having left, in a sorry state, such issues as daycare, equal pay, job designation by gender, discriminatory pension and insurance programs, maternity leave, and job promotion problems.

If such issues are allowed "to slide," women will conclude that the union is not serving their interests and they may not become involved in union activities. Below we trace the hospital workers' contract changes after 1971 up to the strike settlement in 1981 to determine whether there were substantial improvements or deep-seated problems. In Chapter 5 we evaluate the strike's effect on the union's attitude toward women's issues by analyzing the contract before the strike and the one arbitrated in 1986.

Structure: How the Union Does its Work

The major activities associated with union activism include regular union meetings, special union meetings (i.e. conventions), executive or steward activities, and negotiations. Most union meetings are scheduled when the majority of members are *not* working. This after-hours orientation brings women members into conflict with other responsibilities. If union committees, executives, and even senior steward meetings were held during work with pay losses made up either by the employer or union, such an arrangement would diminish the constraints on women members by lessening the conflicts with home responsibilities.

The lack of adequate childcare is another serious problem. The newly formed Ontario Council of Hospital Unions provides child care during conventions. This allows women to engage in union events that they may not have even considered previously. When the time arrives to apply for delegate status at a convention or an educational, the knowledge that children can be cared for, *if necessary*, will encourage participation. If women face constraints on their participation, in union activities they will often not pursue activism because "others have more time." Instead of competing for union positions, women may acquiesce to males whom they feel have more opportunity to do a good job (see Guberman 1983).

The regularity and number of meetings is also a problem for women. The "male model" of unionism allows meetings to be called on short notice, changed with little warning, or extended on the spot. All this affects the longer-range planning a woman faced with a "triple day" has to do.

Kate Purcell (1979: 129) describes unions as clubs with a "homosocial" atmosphere. This is echoed by Guberman (1983) who argues that unions are often sect-like social formations with specialized language and customs. This atmosphere becomes magnified in conventions or negotiation meetings. The structure of these meetings reinforces the "maleness" of these events and deters women's participation. Conventions are usually several days long and are held in cities other than the place of residence. The involvement of women is predicated on family support and services being available. Women also find negotiations even more difficult. Negotiating teams often have little advance notice of extended bargaining. It is not unusual to spend weeks closeted in hotels. The problems associated with this are evident.

These are just a few examples of the problems that deter women from union participation. Interviewees in our study expressed reservations about these issues. Comments such as:

> ...conventions are for the younger girls. I can't take the pace and my family is just as happy. (RNA, Hamilton)

> I don't know how the central negotiators do it cooped up for days talking. The men can handle that, I couldn't. (Housekeeper, Hamilton)

> I did negotiations one year. It is exciting in a way. Would I do it again? I can't. I'm married now and have a boy. (Laboratory Technician, Hamilton)

The formulation varies but the essence remains. The organization of union work presents difficulties for women. The women who can take part are young and childless. This view, expressed by Ontario hospital workers, also corresponds to the information about the problems faced by women unionists in Quebec (Guberman 1975) and the national data presented by White (1980).

Women in CUPE Hospitals

The preceding sections have dwelt on the difficulties, problems, and criticisms of unions from women members' perspectives. Deterrents to participation by women existed in the hospital locals we studied. We can see this from the comments made by the workers as to why women took part in the strike.

Why, then, did women so massively support their union's action? The answers are complicated. Women had specific reasons for supporting the strike *and* reasons that they shared with their union brothers. Several of these emerged from the interviews:

First, the action was a local one. Both male and female unionists identified their own local as the union. While "hospital workers" were "all in it together" and felt a comradery, the strike was a local-based phenomenon. The attitude to middle- and upper-levels of CUPE was negative. Members did not identify with the larger union and, prior to the strike, saw CUPE, at the national level, as part of the enemy. A senior union member at Chedoke repeatedly referred to "them and us," "CUPE versus the union."

Second, as noted above, women had particular reasons for wanting to take action. These were issues pertaining to personal pride, quality of health care and the control of work, to name a few. The difficulties women faced in participating in the regular union functions made the strike a possible avenue to deal with these problems.

Third, the ban on strikes, imposed through legislation, and compulsory arbitration had destroyed bargaining. With the bargaining mechanism closed and the traditional informal pathways (such as talking to supervisors, etc.) ineffective, both men and women, had little choice but to strike. One housekeeper, commenting on the strike, noted:

> Things had gone too far. We talked about it—it had to stop. Our pride was involved, a part of our life was involved. You can't just complain and blame them—you do something.

WOMEN AND COLLECTIVE ACTION

The notion that women avoid collective action, are non-militant and acquiescent in union-management struggles is widespread (see Purcell 1979; Sharpe 1984; Pollert 1983; Edwards and Scullion 1982; Simpson 1981) but is unsubstantiated. There is little or no basis for claiming that women are generally more passive and more acquiescent workers.

Conditioning and Socialization

There are two sources that one can look to for any verification of the "passive women thesis." The first consists of the various psychological tests—which find that men are aggressive and competitive while women are nurturing and cooperative. This thinking was spawned in part by the territorial studies and innate aggression theories popular in the early 1970s. They also arose due to the psychological testing popular in the period. Purcell (1979: 114) makes a persuasive criticism of these tests when she notes:

> ...such findings of differences in the *average* scores of men and women become reified as *sex* differences despite the extensive overlap found between men and women.

It is not possible to sort out the effect of conditioning and socialization in the selection of, what are seen as, appropriate answers. It is not possible to gauge the gender specific reactions to the tests (Purcell 1979).

The other major source of justification is "everyday" common sense. Logically speaking, Purcell argues, the sexual division of labour makes wage work secondary to housework. Less commitment to work, in turn, produces less militancy. But as we described earlier, women are entering the labour force in large numbers for permanent jobs based on economic need. Women's attachment to work is certainly similar to men's and considerable evidence suggests that women are taking less time out of work for family responsibilities. Whereas it was common in the past for women to leave the work force at the birth of the first child and return to work when their youngest child was five, women are now taking only short breaks and returning quickly (Denton 1984: 154). In an analysis of Canadian survey results, it was found that 54.3% of the working women employed in the state sector took no career interruptions (Denton 1984: Table 6–7). In the core sector this was even greater: 61.4% never took any career interruptions. Of the less than half who did experience interruptions, the majority were back in the same work and had stayed for extended periods since the break.

Studies which contradict the assertion of sex-based passivity have also emerged. Sue Sharpe's (1984) British study of working mothers rejects this thesis of acquiescence. While labelling the whole notion of sex-based passivity a social myth, she acknowledges that women, due to pressures at home, find militancy difficult. Kate Purcell's investigation concludes: (1) women act according to the traditions of the industry, not according to their own background or gender (1979: 114); (2) the myth of passivity and non-militancy arises because of women's political invisibility (1979: 113); and, (3) the sexual division of labour creates relative disinterest in work outside the home.

Sharpe finds that in certain situations there is a reluctance among women to take action. In care-giving jobs, they are reluctant to abandon their responsibility or potentially hurt their charges. Yeandle (1984) concludes that women are not more passive but more careful. Woman workers will seek out all the methods available, such as informal consultation, before resorting to strikes. A strike would be more of a final method of resolving problems in the workplace. Gray (1985: 19) and Pollert (1981: 208) note that women engage in strike action *despite* union leaders' expectations that they are passive. Similar findings are reported by Westwood (1984: 67) and Cavendish (1982: 117).

Finally, the sheer numbers of strikes in the late-1970s and 1980s which were led by women speaks against the passivity thesis. The list of strikes with all or a majority of women includes: Fleck (auto parts, Ontario, UAW, 1978); bank workers (UFCW/CUBE); hospital workers, Irwin Toys (Toronto, late 1970s); Eatons (RWDSU, 1984–85); Blue Cross (UAW, 1978); Sandra Coffee; and Puretex.

Why Did Women Hospital Workers Take Action in 1981?

It is difficult to get a clear picture of the differences between men and women in the 1981 Ontario hospital strike. But despite striker's murky memories on this subject, several facts emerge. Both women and men report that women were solidly active in the strike activities; they were more active "than expected."

> Oh no, there was no problem with women on the line. Arrive on time, leave on time—not afraid either. Some of the boys were more nervous. (Maintenance worker, Interview, Hamilton 1986)

The women unionists took initiatives setting up picketing schedules, organizing phone trees, and coordinating refreshments and food. Not one interviewee claimed or recounted any difficulties peculiar to strikers being women. A folklore of short stories recounting "brave women exploits" has developed. The unionists involved in the strike believe women were undaunted, skillful, and to an extent more reliable than their brothers.

The valid points about the deterrents to action which women face apply to the case at hand, but not in the way one may think. The strike took place despite the many deterrents to it.

The explanation involves an examination of a combination of factors. The conditions that brought women to the work force played a role. The question of how work was organized, the changes in the labour process, also had an effect. This included pushing workers out of care situations, the speed up and cutbacks, and changes in assignment. The diminishing rewards and the perceived deteriorating standards of health care all pushed workers toward a strike. Robin Badgely (1975: 10-14) had noted years earlier that there had been and would be strikes in the women-dominated health care systems. He attributed this to an increasing "...awareness of women's rights, the impact of inflation and the disenchantment with the traditional prestige symbols." He also noted that the non-professional health care worker "...makes an effective contribution to patient care" yet is not remunerated for it. The health care workers will strike, argued Badgely, if the need to protect their role in this system is evident.

In our study the perception of the deterioration of the role of the worker in the system is evident. The bond to care-giving work, loyalty to patients, and service orientation created a pressure *to strike*. The need to protect standards impelled women to strike. Women interviewees were asked if they were concerned about the level of care patients would receive during the strike. The most common response involved a defence of the strike *in maintaining health standards*. Typically the hospital worker commented:

> It's them thats wrecked it for people, not us. I can't take care of anyone the way it's set up. That's what I want—to get things back. (RNA, General)

Judy Darcy (1983: 171–79) argues that the denial of the right to strike is a women's issue. She points out that the sectors in Ontario that are denied the strike weapon are dominated by women, i.e. health-care workers, nurses, etc. The hospital workers had to use the strike weapon to fight, what was in the past, women's oppression (Darcy 1983: 177). She adds that the 1981 strike was a conscious and well thought out matter because there was "...a terror campaign organized by the Ontario Hospital Association, the Tory government, and police..." to prevent and then break the strike. For the strikers to carry out such an action in such conditions demonstrates committment.

We noted above that many studies find that women are "careful" about strike action, usually seeking other avenues first. In the hospital strike case, this is born out. The traditional methods of dealing with workplace conflict such as discussion with supervisors, complaints to the department manager, lobbying the head nurse, or negotiating through the union, etc. were all closed.

> Now I know that [...] still listens, she's a good supervisor but like she says it's a new world now. They changed their management thinking and the buck is almighty now. No more listening or thinking about us. (Housekeeper, Hamilton)

Just as the informal mechanisms were being shut down, the arbitration process had severely affected formal bargaining. Those workers interviewed who knew about the contract process repeatedly commented on how negotiations were fruitless or a waste of time.

This left workers with a choice—grin and bear it or take more militant action. The workers opted for action. The strike was a deliberate action consciously decided by a group of unionists, largely women, making a rational decision to attempt to effect changes in their conditions of work.

4

The Strike

There are many interrelated causes for any event. In the case of the 1981 Ontario hospital workers' strike, the multitude of factors that contributed to the action can be divided into two. The first is the complex set of structural determinants that created the condition for collective action. In the preceding chapters we examined these structures. They included a range of fiscal policy and labour control instruments, as well as the form, organization, and functions of the union. The second set of determinants involved the interaction of the participants within these underlying circumstances. Like or similar situations can lead to action in certain circumstances but not in others, depending on a complex of factors such as leadership, history, levels of frustration, and timing, to name a few. In this chapter we examine some causes of the strike that were unique to the participants and their organization.

THE STRIKE: A CHRONOLOGY OF SIGNIFICANT EVENTS

The process leading to the strike and the events during the conflict are complex. The following chronology does not cover everything that transpired but it introduces the reader to the major events discussed later in this chapter:

1. In 1979, at the National Convention of the Canadian Union of Public Employees, delegates voted to defend free collective bargaining and to appoint a full-time coordinator for hospital workers.

2. Peter Douglas, a popular choice for coordinator, was offered the job under conditions which are known to be unacceptable.

3. Bill Brown was appointed coordinator for the hospital work ers. Brown was a staff representative for CUPE who had not originally sought the coordinator position. Brown accepted the coordinator position as a stepping stone to an assignment that he had expressed a long-term interest in—arbitration.

4. The negotiating team was assembled. Patrick O'Keeffe, the Ontario Regional Director, appointed the Assistant Director of the Ontario CUPE Region, Gilles LeBel, to aid Bill Brown in leading negotiations for the hospital workers.

5. September 25, 1980: Brown and LeBel advised the negotiating committee to sign a tentative agreement. The agreement contained increases of 65 cents per hour in each of two years and a long-term disability (LTD) plan. The LTD is secured at the expense of existing sick leave plans which were popular with the workers.

6. September 26: LeBel and Brown put the memorandum of agreement (a tentative contract settlement) before a meeting of hospital local presidents. The agreement was voted down by a vast majority and many local union presidents vowed to fight against it.

7. In the weeks following, union members reviewed the tentative agreement. In late October, the membership of CUPE hospital unions voted 91% to reject the tentative agreement.

8. A new bargaining committee was assembled. Those who supported the tentative settlement were removed.

9. In December, 1980, a conference of hospital workers rejected arbitration, thereby paving the way for a strike vote. The meeting has come to be known as the Rowhampton Massacre because of attacks launched against Brown, O'Keeffe, and LeBel for the perceived "sellout contract."

10. In September 1980, seventy-five percent of the CUPE hospital workers voted for a strike.

11. January 21, 1981: the Ontario Labour Relations Board ordered a halt to preparations for a strike (a cease and desist order).

12. January 21: the CUPE negotiating committee delivered a request for a face-to-face meeting with the Ontario Hospital Association representatives. It requested an indication that

the OHA wanted to begin "give and take" negotiations. The sign was to arrive before late afternoon on January 23, 1981.

13. January 22: Grace Hartman, President of CUPE, speaking for the National Executive, publicly agreed to comply with the order.

14. January 23: Paul Barry (President of the Ajax-Pickering hospital local) and Pat Kenny (member of the negotiating committee) announced at a Toronto rally that strike preparations were to go ahead despite the cease and desist order.

15. A wildcat strike occurred at St. Peter's Hospital in Hamilton. The issue was quality of health care and the endangering of patients.

16. January 23: The union request for negotiations was rejected by the OHA.

17. January 24 weekend: The CUPE negotiating team was prepared to bargain. As a sign of good faith the union committee sent the OHA a revision of all its positions.

18. On the afternoon of January 25, Vic Pathe, the Government-appointed mediator, met with the union committee to announce that the OHA would not bargain under threat of strike.

19. The Progressive Conservatives called a March election. Many commentators claimed the strike was used as a weapon against opposition parties. Informed sources said the Tories thought the Liberals and New Democrats would have difficulty taking a firm stand against the strikers.

20. The strike began at twelve midnight on the 25 of January. In the early morning hours picket lines went up around Ontario.

21. January 26: the Minister of Labour, Robert Elgie, summoned both parties and demanded that negotiations begin immediately.

22. January 26: the Labour Minister created the Disputes Advisory Committee, composed of the mediator, Vic Pathe, Robert Joyce (for the employer) and Terry Meagher, Secretary Treasurer of the Ontario Federation of Labour.

23. Union members reported harassment and intimidation by Ontario Provincial Police.

24. January 27: The Attorney General applied for an injunction against the strike and a back-to-work order.

25. Friday, January 30th: The Ontario Supreme Court granted the injunction.

26. Later, on the 30th, Grace Hartman announced her 100% support for the workers but offered no advice on what to do next.

27. On Saturday, January 31, Roy McMurtry, Provincial Attorney-General, threatened to prosecute union leaders and members.

28. On the morning of Sunday, February 1, the strike committee assessed the future of the strike as poor, with erosion continuing in six areas. Of particular importance was Toronto. Picket lines were "few and far between." Many workers were threatening to return to work and city-wide organization was poor.

29. On the afternoon of Sunday, February 1, the bargaining committee, through the Minister of Labour, made a secret offer to go back to work if there was (a) a promise to begin negotiations, and (b) no reprisals.

30. On Monday evening, February 2, the Toronto strike had collapsed. Kenny, the Toronto negotiator, called for an end to the strike. The OHA refused any conditions.

31. Tuesday, February 3: Hamilton stayed out an extra day.

32. Wednesday, February 4: Hamilton went back to work.

33. March 19: Progressive Conservatives were re-elected.

34. April 6 and 7: Central Arbitration took place.

35. June 1: Paul Weiler, the arbitrator, handed down his award. The wage increase was 80 cents per hour for year one and 85 cents per hour for year two. This represented 35 cents per hour more than what was in the original tentative agreement. The employer's sick leave/LTD package was no longer in place, and other issues such as workload were not improved.

36. In mid-June Grace Hartman, Lucie Nicholson, and Ray Arsenault began their jail term for contempt of court.

THE ORIGINS OF THE STRIKE

The strike did not arise or develop in any standard way. At midnight, January 25, 1981, the strike began and in less than 36 hours over 10,000 workers, mainly women and many immigrants, were on the street. Over 50 of the 65 CUPE organized hospitals were participating. There were many more participants than either the Ontario Hospital Association or CUPE had anticipated. The workers participated despite orchestrated attempts by government, police and the OHA to intimidate them into avoiding collective action. This intimidation included threats of legal action, suspensions, possible firings and personal abuse.

While the government and the hospitals called on workers not to strike, there was little support for the strike from the National Executive Board of CUPE. Some middle-level CUPE officials, including the staff person responsible for hospital unions (Pat O'Keeffe), opposed strike action. And, as the Central Bargaining Committee noted, the strike "...was led not from above but from below. It occurred not because of our leadership but in spite of it" (CUPE 1981: 12). There was virtually no organization of workers at the rank and file level for a strike. Despite all this, a strike with a turbulent aftermath was conducted by workers who were conventionally considered to be passive and intrinsically wed to their "care-giving" work.

The Story Begins

The story of the strike begins at the 1979 CUPE National Convention. By most judgments it was a militant convention. The convention heavily criticized the Canadian Labour Congress President, Dennis McDermott, for not supporting the Canadian Union of Postal Workers' strike. This was a turbulent issue in many unions affiliated to the Congress and Hartman (then President of CUPE) recalls that McDermott made life somewhat miserable for her because of the condemnation from her members:

> You could feel people bristling. Looking back, perhaps Dennis should not have come. It was embarrassing for me the way people went after him and he didn't let me forget the incident.

More importantly, this was the first time hospital workers played an important role in national CUPE affairs. "Hospital workers sort of came of age. They really took part in the debates. It was nice to see," remarked a long-time staff representative.

Along with the many issues of general importance to the hospital workers there were two special convention considerations that would surface over a year later to play a role in the strike.

A call for locals to avoid compulsory arbitration and to fight for the right to strike.

At the National Convention there was agreement on a ground-breaking, 10-point action program. This program was not planned in advance but was drafted at the convention because the rank and file of the union took charge of their convention. The convention was energetic and militant and, amongst other things, called for a fight against all policies infringing on the right to collective bargaining and strikes:

> CUPE will...mobilize all its strength and resources to retain the right to strike and where it exists, to fight against all present restrictions on the full right to strike... (CUPE, National Convention, 1979)

This policy was cited several times during the strike. The Central Bargaining Committee (CBC) evoked it after Grace Hartman ordered CUPE staff and members to obey the cease and desist order in December, 1980. The committee questioned whether this constituted "fighting against all restrictions on the right to strike" as laid out by the convention. In the only union summary of the strike in public, delivered as a speech at the 1981 health-care workers convention, the bargaining committee cited it as one justification for the strike action. It states:

> It is true that this move [the strike] was made against the wishes of the National leadership, but we were adamant that the democratic vote of our members would be upheld. It should be noted that the national policy of CUPE, as adopted by the 1979 national convention, is as follows: "CUPE will...mobilize all its strength and resources possible to retain the right to strike where it exists and *to fight against all present* restrictions on the full right to strike for public employees" (CUPE 1981: 4)

The reluctance of CUPE to launch an all-out offensive against wage controls and constraints in bargaining played an important part in the 1981 hospital strike.

The demand for a full-time coordinator for the 18,000 hospital workers in Ontario.

This demand for a full-time coordinator was the focus of a bitter battle at the convention. Grace Hartman described it as "a battle of wills—it became a symbol for the hospital workers of what they felt was a prejudice from some quarters in CUPE" (Interview, February 24, 1986). The resolution had come three times to the floor for debate before it was passed.[1]

It is clear that hospital workers had received less attention for servicing by the national union than the larger, older, and well-established municipal and hydro locals. Union officers admit the municipal locals may have up to two staff at their disposal plus full-time elected officers. The average hospital local shared a staff representative with a dozen or more other locals. It should be noted here that hospital workers held a relatively disadvantaged position in the union. This stemmed from essentially three factors. First, hospital workers were latecomers to the union; many of the other locals, and particularly the larger municipal locals, had been organized before the 1963 merger that created CUPE. Second, hospitals had, in the past, hired people of varying abilities. (Anne, a long time hospital worker, noted: "They used to hire a certain number of people who may not have been hired outside the hospital. You know, people who were mentally slow or handicapped. With a little help they did a good job.") This led some in CUPE to characterize the whole sector negatively, arguing that many hospital unionists were below average in abilities. Lastly, the hospital workers had several visible spokespeople who were very vocal and quite abrasive at times.

These prejudices were aggravated and augmented by other factors. The gender composition of the hospital workers was taken to suggest the "soft" nature of the hospital sector. This represents a manifestation of patriarchal attitudes that assumed "...real unions were dominated by men not women. The fact that hospital workers did not have the right to strike reinforced this view that hospitals were women's

---

[1] The common practice in CUPE and many other unions is to have a committee organize resolutions to convention. The committee gives its opinion on whether the resolution should be passed (tabling resolutions with concurrence or non-concurrence). When a resolution comes to the floor for debate the delegates may vote for or against the committee recommendations. If they vote against the committee's recommendation a resolution goes back for a "reconsideration" and the resolution is reintroduced later. In the case of the hospital workers' resolution, the committee proposed to defeat it three times in a row but was overturned by the convention delegates.

work and the locals generally weak" (O'Keeffe Interview, January, 1986).

The eventual victory of the fight to get a coordinator welded hospital workers closer together and stirred up their general frustrations. While in the past, hospital workers had been more content to play a peripheral role, they now played an activist role. Whereas in the past only a couple of activists spoke, now many hospital delegates were speaking. The frustration was over being treated differently and having to fight for something that was obviously needed. The fighting and winning inspired confidence and spurred activity.

The majority of hospital delegates at the 1979 CUPE Convention not only wanted a coordinator, but wanted or expected Peter Douglas to be appointed to the post. He was young, sharp, and appeared to many as competent and militant. He had met many people in the Hamilton region, as he serviced Hamilton hospital locals. Douglas had also been in hospital negotiations on many occasions. This had brought him into contact with union activists in the hospital around the province. His reputation was as one who would not get in the way if people wanted to take action to reinforce demands. The hospital workers were disappointed when Pat O'Keeffe, Regional Director for CUPE's Ontario Division, eventually appointed Bill Brown. Like O'Keeffe, Brown was a dedicated and hardworking unionist, and he was someone closer to O'Keeffe's own image of a union coordinator. Brown was an old-style staffer, originally out of the United Steelworkers. O'Keeffe, by his own admission, had no time for Douglas whom he considered to lack the stuff of a good coordinator. "I never heard him talk of anything positively—he curses the inevitable darkness too." Bill Brown admitted "O'Keeffe saw Douglas as a manipulator" and someone "hard to control." O'Keeffe moved the location of the job to Toronto, a move that appeared to be calculated to exclude Douglas or at least to bring him where he could be watched and counselled.

Hospital workers reacted negatively to the new appointment. Many wrote letters to Hartman opposing the switch.[1] Several key

---

[1] There were many protests but two sprang to mind. From Northern Ontario, Justin Legault wrote on behalf of Northern areas and among others Cathy McQuarrie for Toronto. Unionists did not criticize Bill Brown. They questioned why *their* choice was not accepted. It was a democratic issue.

actors, such as the Chairperson of the Health Care Workers Coordinating Committee, C. McQuarrie, reacted bitterly. She said she would never talk to Brown nor work with him. Bill Brown recalled that "Around the Regional Office I couldn't even get a mailing list" (Interview, February, 1986).

The dispute over the selection of a coordinator illustrates the tension between the middle-level leadership and the rank and file members in CUPE. The tension was a visible manifestation of the frustration present in the union. Workers did not dislike Brown—the problem was that they were not consulted about the appointment of "their" coordinator. They saw his appointment as a challenge to their authority. The importance of this issue is underlined in the final summary of the strike written by strike leaders. The strike leaders recommended direct rank and file participation in staff selection (CUPE, 1981: 8). We will see later that the national review of bargaining problems in the hospital sector tried to find openings for the rank-and-file membership to have some input into the selection of the person filling these important positions.

The Bargaining Review Committee would later note, in its study of CUPE after the strike, that members had lost control over decisions and staffing. If relations in the union were going to improve, the health-care workers had to have more control over the selection and work of their coordinator (CUPE 1982: 30–1).

The specific situation in the hospital union reflected a larger issue in CUPE. The national office hires and directs staff and the locals they work with have no control over the staff representative. On the other hand, the locals have a very developed autonomy. The locals' independence, with little control of staff, makes the national union seem an outside body. It makes the staff an agent for the national office. This generates friction and frustration.

After appointing Brown, O'Keeffe further fashioned the staff component of the negotiations committee by appointing Gilles LeBel (Assistant Director of Ontario) to assist Bill Brown in negotiations. Both men seemed to fit the "old-style" mold O'Keeffe preferred.

The Process of Negotiations Leading to the Strike

The round of bargaining is described differently by different actors. Brown, the chief CUPE negotiator, felt that the OHA negotiator was interested in negotiations and was honest. The process, for Brown, was hectic and bitter but not fruitless. Others felt the OHA never really gave much.

The reality is impossible to recreate, particularly because the Central Bargaining Committee (CBC) was cloistered for more than the usual length of time. There are not many bargaining reports or meeting minutes to analyze. This was due to a concern with outside interference by those in control. Both O'Keeffe and Brown felt that some members in CUPE wished to subvert negotiations and create a confrontation. One elected negotiator commented in a letter:

> Bill Brown and LeBel were so preoccupied [in] this round (1980–81) with putting down past staffers and committees' work that they didn't really concentrate on the job. They really kept us away from other people and any other ideas.

O'Keeffe disapproved of what he saw as interference by the radical elements, discontented lower level staff, and the national office staff:

> I did, privately and confidentially, object to the national officers [Grace Hartman, President, and Kealey Cummings, Secretary Treasurer] to what I believed was undue interference in the responsibilities and work of both the hospital coordinator and the assigned assistant. (Public Statement, O'Keeffe, 1981: 1)

In an interview he explained that the Research Department and Department of Organization had tried to interfere in negotiations in the hopes of encouraging a breakdown in bargaining and a subsequent strike. He claimed that the "organization department was quite involved you know. Along with research they manipulated many hospital workers...MacMillan [head of organization] represents a form of extremism in the union" (Interview, February, 1986).

Bill Brown echoed this criticism and cited other problems: "I know they [research department people] were coming into town [Toronto] to meet with the left...Research wanted a strike in the worst possible way...MacMillan's outfit was talking behind my back" (Interview, March, 1986).

Paul Barry, the leader of the opposition had no recollection of any contact with national staff concerning the 1980–81 round before the memorandum of agreement was signed. Gil Levine, former director of the Research Department, unequivocally denies any involvement in the process.

Aside from these alleged interferences, in September, 1980, it became clear there was room to settle. A meeting of Hospital local presidents was scheduled for September 26. This would provide, according to LeBel, a forum to float a memorandum of agreement. Brown concluded an agreement with OHA negotiator Bass. Brown felt this was the best he could do if he was to avoid arbitration and a strike. He stated subsequently: "I wish I'd not have signed it."

Brown confided to friends that he wanted this "awful round of bargaining" to end. His health was deteriorating and his resolve was nearly spent. His closest associates and confidants advised him not to put up with the pressure of criticism, personality clashes, and in-fighting; he should get out. In 1986, Brown commented retrospec-tively that he really wanted the tentative agreement to "go out" and be *rejected*:

> "I didn't need that crap, you know. I thought my heart was going to go. I was sick...Despite all of that I had a plan to carry things through...I wanted it [the tentative agreement] to go out, be voted down and then we could get back and finish the negotiations...I wanted to see where we were and what people wanted."

In the covering letter to the tentative agreement he and LeBel wrote: "In view of the fact that the strike option is...neither feasible nor obtainable...the arbitration process...has not and isn't serving the best interests...We *unhesitatingly* and *enthusiastically* recommend to you that the memorandum be accepted" (Brown, LeBel, October, 1980).

Reaction to the memorandum came from both inside and outside CUPE. The local presidents at their October 26 meeting condemned it. Friends from outside later wrote to criticize it. The Ontario Nurses Association (ONA) wrote:

> For some time now, a number of unions have been acutely aware of the inability to make inroads in our rounds of bargaining...because of what, in our opinion, were premature settlements by one union [referring to Al Hearn and SEIU]. This time CUPE itself disregarded the interests of hospital workers.

The ONA went on to criticize directly many aspects of the memoran-dum.

For Bill Brown and Gilles LeBel, there were few friends at this point. Even O'Keeffe, a staunch supporter of Brown, had some coarse words. He had early on given Brown some of his "old Irish" trade union advice. "You must pick the leader of your committee, the one strong enough for the others to listen to. If that man signs, the rest will. I told him don't sign without Pat Kenny." Pat Kenny was a Toronto representative on the committee and, as such, held a great deal of influence. He had been an activist and local president for many years.

As it turned out, Brown did sign the memorandum without Pat Kenny. Kenny had said he may sign but slipped away to relax before actually doing so. When he returned, much later, he was belligerent and said he wouldn't sign—"it's a sellout," he claimed. Jerry Jones, who represented the Ottawa area hospitals, had also signed but now says, "almost immediately I knew it was wrong," and he was critical of himself later in front of the members he represented in Ottawa.

Brown's support had dwindled. He took the memorandum into the presidents' meeting on September 26. The reaction was electric. The presidents of the hospital workers' locals overwhelmingly rejected the memorandum of agreement. Worse than that for Brown, O'Keeffe, and LeBel was the perception of a sellout that hung around them. Paul Barry, who later became a strike leader, ripped his copy in half as he spoke about its sellout nature. He expressed the majority opinion. The presidents felt "they were part of an end run; that they were being used to slip a bad contract through" (Ully Venohr, President, Chedoke Hospital CUPE Local and negotiating team member). That perception would haunt the staff involved for a long time.

Meetings were held across Ontario, and with the help of the Research Department evaluations of the package, it was rejected by 91%.

The Rowhampton Massacre

The Rowhampton Massacre is a macabre name for a membership meeting held to discuss the Brown memorandum. This meeting provides the first and only hard evidence of any "outside interference." The national Department of Organization chief, Lofty MacMillan, was strong in his rejection of the memorandum. He also pledged strike support. CUPE hospital delegates gathered in early November, 1980, to discuss how to proceed, given the rejection vote. It was a fiery meeting. Lofty MacMillan and Peter Douglas were the only popular staff members there. Other staff members were strongly criticized for their parts in procuring the memorandum of agreement. As a result of the meeting, the Coordinator's power was reduced but he was not banished. When the "dust settled," two other matters were decided: (1) hospital workers would strike in January, 1981; and, (2) a partially-reconstructed bargaining committee would go back to the table with a mandate to begin bargaining again with the *original* demands.

The consequences of this meeting were many. First, there was a distrust between different forces in the union which ranged beyond personalities. The most serious split was in the staff. Second, among the bargaining committee members, there was a serious distrust of the old members who signed the first memorandum. The decision to go back to the original demands was also fateful. This move allowed the Ontario Hospital Association to interpret the whole process as a manoeuvre *designed* to legitimize a strike. From this point on, the OHA refused to negotiate, calling the strike threat intolerable black-mail (Campbell, Head of Employee Relations for the Ontario Hospital Association, Interview, 1986).

The Situation Among the Staff: Differences Contribute to the Strike

There was a serious fracture among CUPE's staff. The Ontario Regional Staff Director, Pat O'Keeffe, believed that many of the national office staff and some of those under him "were not interested in getting a contract, they wanted a revolution... The Department of Organization and Research Department stirred things up." (O'Keeffe Interview, 1986). This concern was echoed by Brown who recalled: "These left-wingers wanted to go to war. They wanted to change the system."

When one searches for splits and fissures, one can usually find them. In this case, though, perhaps the most telling is the language people use to discuss the issue. Many still talk of two sides, CUPE and themselves. Venohr, President of the Chedoke Hospital CUPE Local, talks of "the committee versus the union; unionists against the union." Bill Brown says, Research "had taken sides." O'Keeffe speaks of other major actors as, "those who curse the darkness as if it had no place in existence." This problem resulted partly from the absence of free collective bargaining. With no right to strike, the more traditional (the old-style) unionists viewed an illegal strike as unreasonable. For them, a strategy that optimised gains should be employed as the potential losses were too great.

The newer style of unionists sought to expand the field for bargaining by challenging some of the limiting structures. This involved challenging compulsory arbitration and the ban on strikes. One illustration of the split and tension occurred when the entire servicing staff met to adopt a position on the strike. Staff members are all hired by the National Office. They convened a meeting prior to the scheduled membership meeting at the Rowhampton. The aim was to sort out how they would react to calls for a strike and discuss the criticisms being directed against the tentative agreement. Two issues were dealt with at the meeting. First, it seemed that invitations to the meeting were selective. Peter Douglas, the favoured staffer for hospital coordinator, and Randy Sykes from the Research Department, were not invited. They had heard of the get-together and showed up to challenge the backhanded politics. Douglas and Sykes had to be admitted.

The second issue discussed involved the possibility of a strike. Brown tried to convince the meeting that there were too many risks. "I don't think we can win a strike," said Brown. "Many people agreed with me but many thought we could [win a strike]... The majority of the [negotiating] team wanted a strike. The majority of the executive wanted a strike. I felt we were going to get clobbered, but who was I to convince them no" (Brown, Interview, 1986). At the meeting, the staff decided they would support a positive strike vote.

The strike vote was called and when returns were in 75% of Hospital workers in Ontario had voted in favour of a strike. This is significant. In the 1979–80 strike vote only 49% had voted in favour. The hospital workers judged this round of negotiations to be more serious.

THE ROLE OF MANAGEMENT IN THE STRIKE

During the months leading up to the strike, it became clear that a settlement would not be forthcoming. It was a classic standoff. The Ontario Hospital Association says: "We were not willing to negotiate under a strike threat." Campbell, the head of the Employee Relations Bureau for the OHA, explains "We [the OHA] thought it was just sabre rattling," and "...we were tired of all the rhetoric. Our position was 'no more blackmail.' We had beaten the UAW in the Blue Cross (an agency owned by the OHA) and we could take CUPE. We wanted to end this pattern of threatening to strike" (Campbell Interview, February, 1986). The whole strike threat had taken the OHA by surprise. Bob Bass, the OHA negotiator, and Bill Brown, CUPE's representative, got along very well at the table. They respected each other and both "dealt fairly." When the situation exploded, "We [OHA] sat back and said, 'What happened here,' there must have been some plan afoot to get a deal in order to use it to get a strike," Campbell, head of the Industrial Relations section of the OHA reports (Campbell Interview, February, 1986).

The speed with which the union locals were informed, rejected the package, and took the strike vote fuelled the OHA's view of a radical conspiracy. "There must have been pre-planning," says George Campbell. "They came out like gangbusters overnight." Despite the OHA's perception, investigation suggests this was not the case. Indeed, the lack of pre-planning may help explain the rapid pace of events. There were no complex structures to slow the preparation process down. Rank and file leaders took their case directly to the members. A second consideration was the depth of feeling by hospital workers in the hospitals.

The OHA was officially blind to the causes of the controversy. To it, "Hoodip (the sick leave plan) was a phoney issue blown out of all proportion." "At one point we offered to change our proposal. The union was not interested" (Campbell Interview, 1986).

The issues of the strike were complex. The official (or stated) reasons for the disagreements included a range of monetary and non-monetary items. One of the most public was the employer's desire to replace local sick leave plans with a central disability and sick plan called "Hoodip." For hospital workers, the substitution was not economically desirable, considering many members had hundreds of days banked in their local plans. Many members saw their banked days as a pension fund because in some hospitals, such as the Hamilton Civic, employees could get half of the unused sick days paid out in cash at retirement.

As the strike approached, the hospitals took the situation more seriously. But, right until the walkout, the OHA felt support would be weak:

> Our reports were that people were not that militant. When it happened, a lot more went out than anyone thought. (Campbell Interview, February 1986)

The OHA claims that the Central Bargaining Committee (CBC) for CUPE didn't want to negotiate in the period before the strike. While interviews suggest that many union members thought negotiations wouldn't lead anywhere, the union bargaining committee made several gestures to indicate that they would stay strike action if negotiations began. The final one gesture was in the closing week before the strike date:

> After three days of waiting, and having had no indication whatso-
> ever from the government-appointed mediator that negotiations
> would begin again, we felt compelled to take action. We decided, by
> majority decision, to deliver an ultimatum: If we had no assurance
> that the employers would meet with us to negotiate by five o'clock
> p.m. on Friday, January 23, we would publicly announce that the
> deadline of January 26 was a firm commitment to a strike, following
> the direction of the strike ballot. In spite of our position that a sim-
> ple phone call from the mediator indicating that negotiations would
> commence again would forestall such a move, the message we re-
> ceived was that the mediator would meet with us at five-thirty p.m.
> on that day; nothing more! (CUPE 1981: 2–3)

Management decided to show clearly that they were unwilling to bargain under the threat of a strike.

Many incidents occurred in the weeks leading to the strike date. Hospital personnel directors and administrators had been threatening union members over strike preparations. Their aim was to intimidate the less active local members. An inside source from the OHA confirmed that this strategy was tried. The following warning from Mr. Dixon, Director, Personnel Department, at the Hamilton Civic Hospital was common:

> The Hospital will regard any strike with the gravest of concern and
> any persons who participate in such activity may be subject to the
> legal and contractual consequences. If you in any way indicate sup-
> port for this unlawful activity, or if you fail to report for work, as
> scheduled, you can expect to be subjected to disciplinary action
> which may include suspension or dismissal.

> We have been given to understand that some of the staff of these
> Hospitals have been threatened if they do not take part in this illegal
> strike. One case is already under investigation. Any staff receiving
> similar threats are asked to call the Personnel office where appropri-
> ate action, with police involvement, will be taken. (Dixon, Corre-
> spondence to Employees, January 22, 1981)

Such tactics seemed to backfire. Many workers felt they were denied, on all fronts, their rights. Now management was threatening them for talking about a job action. Far from scaring off less active unionists, it pulled many of the less committed into the process of preparing for the strike.

Some management tactics aimed at discouraging workers and preparing for a strike provoked members into protest. At one Health Centre in Hamilton, the administrator planned a forced evacuation of patients. The hospital management hoped to transfer the elderly patients to various nursing homes in Southern Ontario by using the DARTS bus service, a private bus company subsidized by the Government to transport people with serious handicaps. DARTS also has a CUPE local. The distances were not always short. Some patients were traced to locations as far away as Simcoe. On orders from management, they were whisked away with no warning to the unionized staff caring for them. This was supposed to accomplish two things. First, the workers would not have time to protest. Second, the staff would be shaken by the action and their resolve to strike weakened. It quickly became a fiasco. As relatives arrived to visit, they found empty beds and scattered personal effects. Many relatives panicked when they couldn't find their loved ones. Family members became even more agitated when staff couldn't tell them where their friends and relatives were. In certain cases, according to the union, patients were whisked away without their medication. Workers stated the situation was pandemonium. The hospital staff moved to block the evacuation. The majority of the unionized Darts drivers, upon learning of the circumstances, refused to handle the patients.

The first walkout was underway, as a wildcat, in Hamilton. Probably the collective action would have taken place on a similar timetable with or without the intimidating actions by management, but the intimidation agitated the union members. Some interviewees report they became convinced there was no choice but to strike *because* management took these actions.

The hospital management had a stronger card to play—the law itself. Unfortunately, from the management's point of view, the Labour Minister continued in his view that if the strike could be settled without force all interests were served.[1] The OHA was infuriated. It wanted "more action." After the strike began, the hospitals "...told him [the minister] repeatedly that he had a responsibility to force people back and end the strike" (OHA Official, Interview, 1986).

---

[1] This involved his own office as well as the establishment of a three-person committee made up of Robert Joyce, a management-oriented industrial relations specialist, Vic Pathe, the Government Mediator, and Terry Meager from the Ontario Federation of Labour. The OFL was criticized for being "coopted into a position of objective 'mediation', trying to pour oil on troubled waters," (CUPE 1981: 5) instead of fighting for the right to strike.

However, as the OHA was criticizing the Labour Minister, the Solicitor General and Attorney General were preparing "to come down very hard" on the strikers.

THE STATE WEARS A UNIFORM

The field of action for individuals is restricted by several mechanisms. One of these mechanisms is the setting and enforcing of laws. Essentially, there were two ways in which this was carried out in the 1981 strike. The first was in regulating collective bargaining:

> The Ministry of Labour was promoting mediation in the early days of the strike. Elgie [then Labour Minister] had a notion that the thing could be settled. With the election being called during the strike there were differences of opinion on what the voters would approve. Elgie thought a quick, peaceful settlement would leave relations in the hospitals less damaged and would look good for the government. (Conservative Advisor Interview, January, 1986)

The second approach was more hawkish. According to the union, the Ontario Provincial Police (OPP) played the role of a divisive force aimed at intimidating the strikers. Official summaries note:

> ...OPP officers were photographing pickets, threatening phone calls were being made to members, Union officers were appearing before a judge on contempt-of-court charges and the Attorney General was seeking an injunction against the strike. (CUPE 1981: 9)

Investigation suggests that these are not idle comments made by a strike committee interested in "feathering its own nest." A Toronto activist comments:

> I got a call saying the police was comin'. I never been in trouble before. I was scared. I light a candle and sit in the living room—lights out—peekin out a corner. They came, but I didn't answer the door. I remember just sittin crying and wondrin what next? (Interview, November, 1985)

> It was the second time I'd been summoned to court. I had to look like it didn't bother me—you know—the other girls would get even more upset if I seemed scared. I was getting upset though. I didn't know what they could do to me. (A Hamilton Strike Leader, October, 1985)

Vic Pathe, the chief mediator, warned the negotiating committee throughout the first week that Elgie would soon not be in charge and that some members of the Provincial Cabinet were "fixing for a bloodletting." The Solicitor General allegedly told the chief CUPE negotiator in the first weekend of the strike, "There will be law and order, Mr. Brown, and you don't represent law and order (Interview, 1986).

The Ontario Supreme Court injunction against the strike was slow in coming. It was not released until Friday, January 31. Many argue that this slow process suggests that there was some hope of getting a non-legislated end to the strike. It is possible that the courts were delaying the decision in that hope. However, the fact that the decision was imminent had a deterrence effect on the strikers.

For the provincial government and hospital authorities, the stakes were getting higher. Could the laws of the duly-elected government be flaunted? Could any government running for re-election afford to appear so weak and open to challenge. These, or similar questions, must have plagued the Conservative government in Ontario.

The Supreme Court finally granted the injunction against the strike on Friday, January 30. McMurtry, the Attorney General, gave the clearest statement of the ideological implications of this strike. He stated publicly that:

> The Supreme Court has once again confirmed the Attorney General's role as Protector of the Public Interest... Once again I must stress the importance of the role of the Ministry of the Attorney General in bringing an end to lawlessness... I am convinced that the majority are law abiding citizens and that many participants are being swept away by leaders who portray their cause as being more important than respect for the law. I am appealing to the usually law abiding citizens who do perform a very valuable public service in our hospitals not to diminish their status in their community by illegal behaviour. I urge them not to be misled by the union leaders whose priorities do not at this time appear to include the real interests of the workers whom they are elected to serve. Any breach of law is serious but mass defiance of the law shakes the very foundation of a civil society.... Respect for the law simply reflects the fact that we cherish our free society. (Roy McMurtry, Attorney General, 1981)

The Attorney General's statement attempted to justify the injunction in the necessary task of maintaining legitimacy for law, and hence for society. The Government's need to protect health care was also evoked:

> Hospital workers are prohibited by law from striking. The legislation was passed by representatives of all the people to ensure that the health of the public is protected. (Roy McMurtry, Attorney General, 1981)

Although McMurtry raised this issue, OHA representative, Dixon, later admitted there was never any danger to patients (Personal Letter to William Powell, Hamilton Mayor, March 1981.)

All of this occurred against the background of a forthcoming provincial election. Some senior trade unionists in the province felt the Government wanted to use the strike to show it could be tough with labour. An analyst for the Conservatives commented there was hope [among Tories] that the NDP or Liberals might have come out sounding pro-strike. In that case, the Tories could have used the "protection of health" argument to discredit them. If the NDP and Liberals didn't come out, then they might lose the support of Labour. "Each scenario served the Tories." (A Progressive Conservative, Interview, 1986.)

THE STRIKE COLLAPSES

The strike surpassed most union members' expectations in its early days. The initial 30 hospitals on strike reached a high of 52 establishments, a positive accomplishment for the union. The major weak spot was in Toronto where the strike collapsed (according to many unionists) because there was insufficient leadership. There was only one staff representative for the city of Toronto.

Several staff members think ethnicity played a role in the weak support in Toronto. The relatively large number of immigrant workers in Toronto hospitals may not have been properly organized to participate. There was no translation of materials, no representation from different ethnic groups on decision-making bodies, and generally no effort to involve immigrant members in the strike. But there is no evidence that any particular immigrant grouping played a negative role in the strike. Similarly, there is no evidence that women were reluctant participants. Quite the opposite is true. Women were the backbone of this strike and immigrant women played a large part. In some places such as St. Joseph's Hospital (Toronto), Portuguese women arrived with eggs and kept trucks from crossing the picket line for days. Every picket captain or local strike committee person interviewed made the same comment. "We were worried that some of the women, especially immigrants, would not participate. We were wrong: overnight duty, 7:00 a.m. or 11:00 p.m. women were out and picketing."

Whatever the reasons, Toronto collapsed. The negotiating committee had knowledge of this on Sunday, February 1. In their regular conference telephone call, committee members agreed to seek a peaceful return with no reprisals. This had been in preparation for days. CUPE had, as early as Friday, January 30, said privately that a new offer and a no-reprisals clause would end the strike. But on Sunday the union dropped its demand for a new offer and instead demanded a guarantee of resumption of the collective bargaining. An informant among the hospital association members commented to a senior CUPE officer: "They wanted blood; an unconditional settlement and there would be retaliation."

By Monday, February 2, the provincial strike was non-existent. Much of Toronto was back and demoralization was setting in amongst locals in other areas of the Province. This new strike committee decided to go back. The members in such places as Hamilton, Ottawa and Sudbury were shocked:

> I couldn't believe it. I was in shock. I remember sitting down on the wet grass and snow and crying my eyes out. (Housekeeper, Hamilton)

> When the girl came up and said it's over I said get lost. She must be a management turncoat—but the news came over the radio...my stomach was all tied up—you know. (Dietary Worker, Hamilton)

Many rank and filers immediately blamed the union:

> I knew they had sold us out. All along them had done everything they could to sell us out. Hartman orders us to desist the strike, that Keefe (*sic* O'Keeffe) guy tries to stop us—ah what chance is there? (Maintenance Worker, Hamilton)

The "surrender" reinforced the rank and file distance from the union. Members knew Grace Hartman had early on ordered members to obey the cease and desist order; they knew many people, such as O'Keeffe, had opposed the strike "all the way along," and they knew the first settlement that was signed was unacceptable. The folding of the strike with no protection against retaliation fueled the view that the union's upper level had sold out the strikers. On the other hand, many of the rank and file hospital workers we interviewed regarded the strike differently than those in middle leadership. They did not regret the action, even when it meant suspension:

> We had to go, it really wasn't a choice you know. I can't tell you why exactly except they had to be shown we'd been pushed just that much too far. We have pride, we work like humans not dogs.

> We needed to say to ourselves and them, things got to get better!
> (Older Female Striker)

The hospital worker's frustration had been "heated to boiling" and the strike gave back some feelings of decency and respect. Some typical comments:

> If we hadn't struck no one would ever have listened. (Housekeeper, Hamilton)

> It was a necessity, it brought us back to life, it restored my pride. (Dietary Worker, Hamilton)

> We may not have gotten the demands but that's not why I was there. Things would be even worse if we hadn't gone out—I have no regrets. (RNA, Hamilton)

Following the collapse of the strike, there were thousands of suspensions and several firings. The OHA wanted to show, first, that a strike threat would have no positive consequence and, second, that there were negative consequences to going outside the established industrial relations structure. George Campbell, Director of Personnel and Industrial Relations for the OHA, put it bluntly:

> We could never give in regardless. The future would have been worse and worse....if you reward illegality you will get it back even worse... If CUPE's thing had been a success others would have looked up and said that's the way to go... (George Campbell, OHA Interview, 1986)

At a meeting of hospital administrators in the OHA, it was decided that each hospital would take its own measures. The decision was that there should be suspensions and firings. Individual managements would determine who would be fired or suspended and for how long. (Interview with hospital administrator)

The extensive and diverse penalties "...showed how angry administrators were about the walkout," says Campbell of the OHA. They also show how divided administrators were over the "evil" of civil disobedience. Some hospitals, such as Joseph Brant (Burlington), gave out a few reprimands, while others such as the General in Hamilton gave out hundreds of suspensions. The penalties were many, but not as major as appears at first glance. John Deverell, the *Toronto Star* reporter who functioned as a conduit for news, claimed that in all Ontario "Thirty-four were fired, while 3,442 CUPE members received suspensions totalling 8,646 days" (Deverell, 1982: 3). Of the thirty-four fired, all won their jobs back through arbitration. For some, the suspension lasted for 18 months.

This strike took place. There was no preparation for an encounter. There was no prior education nor strike material prepared. "The fact that it succeeded as well as it did is a credit to the hospital workers" (Levine Interview, 1989).

The Aftermath: Examining The Effects of the Strike

RETALIATION

It is common after an emotion-filled strike action that a "no retaliation" or "no reprisal" clause be part of the back-to-work agreement. After the 1981 hospital strike, the hospital administrations, coordinated by the OHA, handed out a severe set of penalties. One hospital administrator confided "...there was a lot of animosity toward the union. Several of the administrators were adamant that we go for blood." CUPE and the more militant workers in the various locals had to be taught a lesson, according to some in the OHA. The lesson included a wide range of penalties. Thirty-four workers were fired and 3,442 were issued suspensions for varying periods. Many were a few days or weeks and some were over a year long.

The union had argued for a "no reprisal" clause but the arbitrator, Paul Weiler, took the following position:

> ...the last request made by CUPE by this Arbitration Board was that we award a "no-reprisals" clause, one which would be inserted in the collective agreements of each of the Hospitals. This would ban, retroactively, all discipline of any kind for any employee involved in the illegal strike, and would also require withdrawal of all judicial, quasi-judicial and similar legal proceedings.

> Essentially, the theory of the Union is that a no-reprisal clause is standard fare at the end of any emotion-laden strike, that the only reason why none was agreed to here is that the weight of the law ended their strike, and thus this Board—whose mandate is to reproduce the results of free collective bargaining—should impose the provision on the Hospitals... I am not persuaded by the Union's claim that its members are entitled to full immunity for their illegal course of conduct. Even besides the obvious concern to maintain the incentive to comply with the law generally, a hospital strike can be a

dangerous experience for the patients whose health is risked as a rest. Whatever everyone's views about the relative merits of the policy embodied in the *Hospital Labour Disputes Arbitration Act*, it is terribly important that this system be respected while it still remains the law...

That does not imply that there should be no limits to the scope of discipline... There is a natural tendency in such an emotional, highly-publicized conflict for the employer to over-react. Even worse,...some employers will be restrained but others will not be... In this case, for example, of the seven members of the Union's Provincial Negotiating Committee, a body which clearly played a senior role in development of the strike action, every person received a different form of discipline from their respective hospital employer: ranging from a pure reprimand, to suspensions of two to seventeen days, up to a single discharge. After...reviewing the legal arguments made by the Hospitals, I am not persuaded that this interest arbitration Board does have jurisdiction to deal with the reprisals issue in the first place. Thus, while I believe there is some force in the points made by CUPE, I believe these concerns are going to have to be addressed in the grievance arbitration system to which many of these discharges are not en route. (Weiler 1981)

The position illuminates several of the theoretical propositions we mention later. Weiler is clear that the legitimacy of the system is the key reason why there must be retaliation: "...it's terribly important that this system be respected." This is also the position the Attorney General put forward (see Chapter 4). In arguing that he will deny protection in order to protect the legitimacy of the law, Weiler claims the arbitration cannot act on the reprisals due to the legal limits placed on it. This is a paradoxical position. While collective bargaining is regulated by law, the law cannot deal with the consequences of legal interference in industrial relations.

Weiler's decision also became the jurisprudence for other individual arbitrations aimed at reducing suspensions or gaining reinstatement. Ken Swan, arbitrator for *St. Peter's Hospital vs CUPE Local 77*, stated in June, 1981:

I am relieved that Professor Weiler did not take the action to which he was so nearly persuaded [i.e.]...a general amnesty. (p. 30)

Swan went on to state that discharge was too severe but six month suspensions were reasonable in the St. Peter's case due to the wildcat strikes (p. 34). In doing so, he and Weiler set a path which the other arbitrations followed. The arguments that Weiler and Swan based their case for severe discipline were patient danger and illegality. However, as noted earlier, there was no *demonstrated* danger to patients, and the illegality could have been left to the Government to pursue. After more than a year of legal wrangling, the dismissals were all reversed. The suspensions were upheld and the hardship to many union members was extensive. Typical was this comment:

> It was hell, no pay, maybe no job and it dragged out endlessly. I nearly went over the edge. (Interview, Hamilton)

There was a serious imbalance to the penalties. Paul Barry, a strike leader, was reprimanded. Pat Kenny, a person of equal culpability, was fired. Some hospitals issued 5–10 day suspensions and/or attached letters to personnel files (e.g. Scarborough), according to union sources, whereas other hospitals, such as the Ottawa Perley, seemed to declare war on the strikers:

> Local 870 suffered the worse reprisals of any participant in the 1981 strike. While the strike was still in progress, THIRTY-SEVEN workers were laid off. Following the return to work, EIGHT union leaders were fired. The original reason given for the layoffs was bed closure due to renovations, but no substantial renovations were ever done, and no beds were closed.

> None of the fired workers are back at work. No offers of settlement have been made, and the employer has used every possible means at its disposal to frustrate the union's attempts to defend their members, including judicial review.

> The Local has not taken all this lying down; four local rallies have been held, with good local support, in order to show the management that obvious union-busting will not go unanswered. In response, the hospital has permanently laid off another TEN workers, and hired twenty-one nursing students. (CUPE, local 870 Newsletter, 1981)

The Health Care Workers Coordinating Committee (HCWCC) conference in the fall of 1981 characterized the management reprisals as "vicious, probably the worst large-scale example of union-busting in decades" (Paul Barry, Report: 1981: 9). The final act was the jailing of three senior CUPE officials, including President Grace Hartman. This largely symbolic act can only be understood as the state's need to assert its control and authority. It was an act of legitimization. To the vast majority of interviewees, the punitive moves were a sign of weakness and created an even more sour industrial relations climate.

EFFECTS ON THE UNION'S STRUCTURE

The union's structure was changed after the conflict as a result of membership and official dissatisfaction. In this section we will explore CUPE's form and method of organization and trace the changes that took place inside the union.

Union Organization

John Deverell (1982: 4) places considerable emphasis on what he views as CUPE's "obvious weaknesses." These include:

> (a) a multiplicity of elected positions barren of power; (b) powerful staff positions, notably the regional directors, unaccountable to an electorate; (c) dues paid to locals and remitted to the central organization, leading it to be preoccupied with fiscal survival and debt collection rather than policy and leadership functions; (d) in the hospital sector, a national servicing staff stretched very thin, unsupported by any locally paid officers.

The implications of these "obvious" weaknesses are not explored by Deverell. The research in our study substantiates some of Deverell's claims. The two general problems that plagued CUPE in the hospital sector were: (1) the lack of democracy and (2) ineffective leadership.

Democracy

The first two points that Deverell makes (including elected persons with little power and very powerful staff) did affect democracy. The multiplicity of levels made interconnections, consultation, and coordination difficult but, more importantly, the structure allowed few opportunities for elected members at the local level to intervene in decision making. Up to the mid-1970s, bargaining was conducted directly between locals and their hospitals. The coordinated bargaining directly with the OHA meant local executive members' role was diminished. Members felt they had little say in bargaining. The exception to this was when, at the invitation of higher-ranked officials, *ad hoc* groups were "pulled in" to make evaluations. In the strike, local presidents had one opportunity, early in the process, to be involved. At the September 26, 1980, meeting in Toronto, they were presented the memorandum of agreement with instructions from the staff to agree to it. The presidents rejected the memorandum of agreement. Bill Brown, the staff representative, had expected the presidents would simply accept it and thereby cut off criticisms of the bargaining process. However, one president who had been there commented:

> There had been a long history for us of not being able to get our opinions heard. When we saw the thing [the memorandum] we blew...I was damned if I was going to shut my eyes anymore...They gave me a shot and I took it. Me and the others said NO!

The problem is a common one. When a senior leadership sets up *ad hoc* structures to involve the lower echelons there appears to be more democratic involvement. But, these transitory, and non-legally binding, *ad hoc* arrangements tend to dilute participation and democracy. In the 1981 case the presidents had the memorandum foisted on them with the hopes of slipping it past so that it might look better to the members at ratification time.

The lack of permanent structures with clearly-defined powers is a democratic issue. These structures are usually referred to as intermediate structures (because they are between members and senior leaders). Explorations of participation and democracy, such as by Warner and Edelson (1976), suggest problems with the practice where legally-constituted forums are not developed. It is seen as a critical element in the subjugation of democracy. Lipset (1956) notes that, if intermediate bodies do not exist and the union officials control communication and organization, "...the members are usually unable to act collectively in dealing with their leaders..." (1956: 77). This in turn reinforces the control of the leadership. The point is not that leadership monopoly necessarily means poor decisions; quite the contrary is often the case. Membership democracy reinforces member involvement and organizational integrity. Without member involvement there will be no new candidates for senior leadership and no mid-level leadership development. In the realm of ideas, the challenge of members weeds out poor proposals and generates new ideas.

The only decision-making body for hospital workers was the Health Care Workers Coordinating Committee (the HCWCC). This was created at the Division (Provincial) level. It had no jurisdiction over bargaining matters and, as several interviewees pointed out, staff did not want the HCWCC getting involved in the bargaining. This committee was largely educational and had limited resources at its disposal. This reduced its power of action as well.

Another problem in the CUPE system was information flow. The staff could restrict information and thereby effectively disenfranchise local members. In 1980–81, there was considerable criticism of the staff responsible for negotiations. During the initial negotiations, a bargaining committee member wrote to another union official to explain:

> They (staff negotiators) are preoccupied with keeping information about how we feel from others in the union. They seem more afraid of being criticised or undermined than they are of management. I'm just not comfortable with the whole thing. There are some people we've been "ordered" not to talk to. (Personal letter from a CBC member)

The fact that staff in CUPE were hired and directed by the national office made abuses possible. The local members had no power to discipline what they may have viewed as improper behaviour. Therefore the elected officers who worked directly with staff had no power or say over what they did. This caused strained relations between staff and members. Workers and local executives came to see the staff as an outside influence. Some interviewees likened staff to a fifth column inside negotiations. Although this was only a minority of people, it indicates the fragile relations within CUPE at the time. The Ontario Director had tremendous power because he or she could control information and direct the actions of the only full-time employees of the union—the staff.

Reinforcing this was the attitude of the National Executive Board. The national leadership expected the Regional Director to maintain control and exercise power in negotiations and related disputes such as the 1981 impasse (Hartman interview, 1986). This is not to say that the National Executive Board wanted local leaders to be left out. But they expected things to proceed with a minimum of controversy. This can often create a contradiction between membership involvement and political expediency.

Ineffective Leadership

We have already commented on the small staff complement which led to poor servicing and poor leadership of the hospital sector by the national union. Three separate criticisms of the union along these lines were made by those in and out of CUPE. These were the lack of systematic strike preparation, the lack of strike coordination, and the lack of adequate information.

Strike preparation was nearly non-existent. Workers' feelings ran high and little training was offered to these first-time strikers. One clerical worker commented:

> I didn't know anything about strikes. I wanted to know so I tried to find out. After I phoned around it was clear to me that either no one knew or the ones who did were impossible to get to. I finally called a friend in another local and they told me there was information in a CUPE manual. I read it over and that's how I learned about picketing and things. (Clerical, Hamilton)

Other unionists also expressed dissatisfaction. An aide commented:

> ...in a union as big as ours I figure someone knew how to run a strike but I'll be damned if I could figure out how to find them.

The additional problem of no clear communication network or educational network increased the difficulties.

A second dimension was strike coordination. Timing is often critical in a strike. Actions have to be coordinated. Those trying to hold things together reported real difficulties, given the lack of a systematic coordinating body.

The third dimension was the lack of information. It was a serious contributor to disunity during the strike. Many union members throughout the Province obtained their news about the strike from the media, not the union. This left them prone to misinformation about the direction the strike was taking. For example, during the strike Toronto was one of the weaker centres. The media "played this up." This produced feelings of failure, led to disappointment in other centres around the Province, and this helped to undermine the strike. An orderly made a typical comment:

> It was depressing. Every night they showed unpicketed hospitals on the tube [television]. Our own president didn't know if Toronto had given up. I know that I found it hard to take! (Orderly, Hamilton)

Members Seek Changes Over the Years

The difficulties with the existing structures had been a constant topic of discussion among local members. This "...can be traced back to the 1974–76 period when bargaining was in flux" (CUPE 1982(a): 2). In 1974, several areas, notably Toronto, began cooperating and bargaining regionally. The larger wage increases won by Toronto (see Chapter 3) reinforced the positive attitude to regional cooperation.

Based on the 1974 negotiations, the hospital workers formed seven regions. The hospital workers moved from a structure where each hospital conducted its own negotiations to a federation of regions en route to full central bargaining. The review of hospital negotiations by the Johnston Commission proposed moving to central bargaining to improve industrial relations (Ontario, 1974: 2). CUPE was already in support of such a move[1] but the OHA was reluctant for a variety of reasons. Despite this, the OHA and CUPE proceeded toward central-ized bargaining on a voluntary (i.e. non-legal) basis. Over several rounds of negotiations, a form of centralized bargaining did evolve. "Although provincial-wide bargaining became a fact, CUPE never adapted its structure to suit the new situation" (CUPE 1982(a)).

The union adopted a regionally-based bargaining committee sim-ilar to a U.S. Senate-style model where each region, regardless of its population, had equal representation. Toronto, for example, had the same number of delegates as the northwest region, despite its mem-bership being nearly ten times larger. This caused problems of un-equal representation.

There were other problems with the Central Bargaining Committee (CBC). The CBC performed an important set of duties outside of bargaining, even though it had no mandate to do so. It was the only body that provided a link between hospital workers. Unfortunately, it functioned only during the period of negotiations. As well, the CBC's membership changed regularly. Between negotiations the committee lacked the ability and desire to coordinate members' affairs. This lack

---

[1] While the 1974 victories on wages prompted a move to more centralized forms of bargaining there were also serious blocks to this shift. The mem-ber locals did not want to give up any superior benefits or "language" in negotiations centrally. This meant CUPE had to demand that any centrally negotiated contracts adopt the best clauses from the local contracts. Such a demand was sure to scuttle early attempts at achieving agreement from the OHA Even tough negotiators, such as Peter Douglas, recognized this as a difficult stumbling block.

of coordination was compounded by a poor system of communications. CBC members had few resources to gather ideas or disseminate information in their local unions. As well, little information travelled between regions. This ensured that, even when the CBC met, the representatives had considerable difficulty sorting out priorities. A collective approach to deciding priorities was also difficult because the constituencies often gave their representatives very explicit instructions, leaving the CBC with little room for compromise.

Another problem, evident in the 1981 conflict, was the lack of authority which the various bodies within the union needed to do their work. In 1981, at the Health Care Workers Coordinating Committee (HCWCC)[1] annual convention it was noted:

> ...As it stands now our presidents meetings and mini-conferences have no constitutional authority... We feel that the approval of a new structure would go a long way toward cleaning up our act. (CUPE 1981)

The new structure referred to is a council of hospital unions that would, in their words, "retain the regions, and ensure local autonomy would be protected while providing a rational and disciplined means of making and abiding by central decisions" (ibid.). This council was to be born out of an internal review prompted by the 1981 strike.

CUPE Investigates Itself: Two Commissions

While nerves were raw, and tempers hot, CUPE's national executive and staff pondered their moves. Two initiatives followed. Shortly after the strike, the Secretary Treasurer of CUPE, Kealey Cummings (the "number two" national leader) appointed Bill Vincer, President of the CUPE Hydro Workers, Local 1000, to investigate what "really" happened during the strike. The "Whitewash Commission," as it quickly came to be known, didn't report until April 1982. Its investi-

---

[1] The HCWCC was a creature of the Ontario division. It was seen by activists as a place where political questions concerning all hospital workers could be discussed but not as a body to alter bargaining structure. The mandate of the committee was narrow and the average rank and file member saw it as "ineffective and a waste of time and money." Subsequently, changes have taken place and it has concentrated on member education and the nursing homes. Members are commenting more favorably about the HCWCC since this shift in priorities.

gation consisted of interviewing 36 people over a two-week period. Vincer blamed everything on personality clashes.

Meanwhile, Grace Hartman accepted the advice of her senior staff directors. Tobachnick (Public Relations), Levine and Sykes (Research), and MacMillan (Organization Department) approached President Hartman urging her to take steps to correct the situation among hospital workers. They suggested that the four of them be constituted as a "Royal Commission" to investigate the strike and make recommendations on what should be done by CUPE to avoid a repeat situation in the future. This coincided with a recommendation from the Health Care Workers Conference which called for a post mortem and a review of the union structure (CUPE, May 1981). To this end, a tentative committee was formed.

This provided the opening the national staff needed. They put convincing arguments to a receptive President. The national staff asked Hartman to give the committee created at the Health Care Workers Conference an official mandate. The committee could be expanded to include a national staff member and other departments would cooperate. Part of the convincing argument, put to Hartman by the central staff, was the threat of a breakaway of hospital workers similar to one that had taken place in British Columbia in the 1970s. President Hartman went one step further than the national staff proposal. She commissioned the "gang of 4" (Levine, MacMillan, Sykes, and Tobachnick) to do the study. Paul Barry was selected from the hospital workers, as were six other elected negotiators. This would ensure tight control, give the committee more voice in CUPE proper, and show that the National Executive Board was serious.

The Bargaining Review Committee's findings were not aimed at the particular battles between individuals during the strike. The committee set out to accomplish two things: (1) give hospital workers a chance to voice complaints; and (2) make recommendations concerning a new structure (interview with Committee Member). The committee began by reviewing the situation in other Canadian jurisdictions. They found many provinces had adopted intermediate bodies; namely, councils of hospitals. Some organizational literature maintains that introducing intermediate bodies tends to blunt participation, reduce democratic challenges, and bureaucratize functioning (see Edelstein and Warner, 1976; Anderson 1981). However, in this case, the aim was different. The upper echelon of leadership, notably President Hartman, wanted to fashion a better position for the hospital workers in CUPE. Several of her senior advisors supported her concern and were convinced that organizational change would increase participation. As we will see below, this was essentially a correct perception.

It was not just senior staff and officers that looked to a new body. The HCWCC conference had endorsed a similar idea. The committee, armed with its research, went on tour. Committee members knew they would have to vent anger, test the council idea, and gather other ideas. In a tour of the Province, locals representing over 80% of the hospital membership were reached and support for the Council was strong. The results of the review committee reveal sets of inter-related and structural problems. Table 5.1 outlines the complaints uncovered and Table 5.2 outlines the recommendations.

The report led to the founding, in 1982, of the Ontario Council of Hospital Unions (OCHU). As we will see in the next section, the Council accomplished or attempted to accomplish many important things. The hospital workers had created a vehicle they could "drive"—one that could more effectively serve hospital workers.

Paul Barry (the rank and file member who emerged as a leader during the strike) was elected president at the 1982 founding convention. OCHU was structured along the lines of the committee's report (see Table 5.2). The organization of OCHU was innovative because it contained many provisions for membership control, such as the recall of officers. The hospital workers were, and are to this day, proud of the structure.

THE ONTARIO COUNCIL OF HOSPITAL UNIONS

Life Inside the Ontario Council of Hospital Unions

The Council's, according to its President, was to become workable and rational. The outcome was to be a body in which hospital workers respected their leadership and the collective decisions. This respect was to be based on democratic functioning and the accountability of that leadership. The prior situation was likened, by Barry, to "...feudal Italy with its city states." The province had been divided into seven regions that did not mesh into a collectivity. In addition, there was the staff problem. The regional director, who controlled all staff, "...often passed by elected people and circumscribed

Table 5.1: Report of Complaints to Hospital Bargaining Review Committee

Structure	Bargaining	Communications	Staff
1. Structure was not working; it had not changed with the move to regional and central bargaining. The federation structure was inadequate.	1. There was a need to improve the centralized bargaining process.	1. There is no system of communications; therefore there are very poor internal communications.	1. Hospital coordinator has been utilized poorly. The lack of a central body for hospitals means coordinator takes on too much.
2. It was impossible to bring locals together with the authority to make decisions.	2. In moving to central bargaining superior benefits and general superior language has to be protected.	2. The lack of a communication system leads to waste because printed material never gets distributed.	2. Staff have too much power and elected people too little.
3a. There was no permanent central decision making group. 3b. The equal representation despite population was undemocratic.	3. The bargaining resolution procedure for local issues is unsatisfactory. After central bargaining there is very little room for local issue bargaining. As well, central negotiators can't understand the importance of local issues.	3. Lack of information is more acute in the small centres, thereby creating splits and animosities.	3. The current hospital co-ordinator (Bill Brown) must go.
4. Smaller regions have on-going financial problems.	4. Bargainers elected locally have their hands tied with local instructions. They are unable to make quick decisions.	4. Hospital workers get more information from the *Globe and Mail*. There should be a newspaper or newsletter.	
5. There was a need for an impeachment or recall provision for leaders.	5. Bargaining is too secretive.	5. All communications have been in English. French and even other languages should be used.	

Table 5.2: Major Recommendations Reported to Hospital Review Committee

Structure	Bargaining	Communications	Staff
1. Move to create a council of Hospital Unions.	1. A policy must be adopted to ensure that local unions will not be forced to accept a reduction in benefits or inferior language as a result of a central bargaining (without their knowledge). Central bargaining committees should not interfere with local bargaining.	1. A proper communications system shall be established which does not rely on the staff but utilizes them. Area Vice-Presidents shall be responsible in large part for that system.	1. In future the coordinator must be selected in consultation with the new council.
2a. The regions will become information bodies for the locals. Their role in bargaining will diminish.	2. A computer data bank with all contracts should be established so negotiators will know whether any hospital has a superior clause.	2. A newsletter shall be established.	2. Coordinators must have high profile in regions.
2b. Council would have responsibility for bargaining and would leave the H.C.W.C.C. the jurisdiction over political issues, at the provincial level, that do not concern bargaining.	3. A protocol between CUPE and OHA should be defined to outline what are central issues and what are local issues.	3. All materials should be published in French and English. Where possible, other language reports should be produced.	3. Coordinators should be primarily involved in negotiations.
3a. There will be an elected leadership that will run the council between conventions.	4. Central bargaining should not be so secretive. Regular reports will be issued to the locals.		4. Each region should have a staff coordinator.
3b. There should be representation by population except in bargaining where the areas each elect a Vice-President which is a member of the executive and on the bargaining committee. This was a compromise position.			5. There must be cooperation between coordinators and national office departments such as research.
4. There should be a recall provision.			
5. One financial commitment will be minimal; 1/10 of 1% and in the process of operation poorer regions will be helped.			

any democracy that might have survived the structural morass" (Barry Interview, 1986).

Since democracy was a key goal of the new executive, it introduced an annual convention. This delegate convention is governed by parliamentary procedure, has representation by population and can replace leaders if delegates so decide. The leadership can be made accountable between conventions as well. Hospital locals are voluntary members of the Council. This keeps the Council executive alert for fear of losing members.

Members of OCHU have reported a dramatic change. A recurring comment from those who had been at conventions was:

> You don't feel intimidated. If you want to talk people let you—and they listen. I trained as an observer so it was easier too. (Interview, Housekeeper, 1986)

The "training" that this housekeeper speaks of is a unique procedure. OCHU encourages each local to send an observer to conventions so that more people could become familiar with procedures. As a result, each year the competency of the delegates improves. This whole package of changes is, in the words of the President, "putting hospital workers in the driving seat of *their* organization." This in turn makes the members responsible for their organization and its function.

> Something you make with your own hands or fix up you know— it's different than what you get pushed on you—you can feel its yours and be proud or if its going bad—you fix it again. (Maintenance Worker, Hamilton)

The Council moved very quickly to get its house in order. Its president began immediately, with support from his newly elected executive, to rebuild or initiate programs in education and communication.

In the realm of communications, the new philosophy of accountability and membership involvement occurs at three levels. First, hospital workers learn about developments and long-range plans through the Council's congress and other permanent bodies. Representatives to the Council are expected to inform their constituents. The second level is a regular newspaper/newsletter. This "press" was created by the new Council executive. It is a readable and topical newspaper that aims to inform and educate. The third level is a systematic mailing system that gets fast-breaking information to members in leaflet or letter form.

Despite an extended "shakedown" period, the communications system has been a great success. None of the interviewees complained of problems and some commented very positively. A typical reaction was:

> Oh sure there's junk but what paper doesn't have some things that are. I'll tell you—I want to decide if its good or bad—before I got nothing—no information. Now I do and that's the way I like it. (RNA, Hamilton)

In the second year of operation, the Council began an innovative education program. It was designed to take activists, and "green" members alike, and give them two types of training. In the footsteps of urban organizers such as Sol Alinsky, the Council provided training on how to motivate and organize others. Several women (and men) interviewees noted:

> I'm still scared but I don't think its half as bad as before...If you told me a year ago that I'd be wandering around with leaflets during break chatting people up about the union I would have laughed. Now I do things...I even gave a talk. (Dietary Worker, Burlington)

The second type of training was basic "nuts and bolts" instruction on steward activities, such as grievances and wider political education on labour legislation and related matters. While these type of seminars were available in the past, their frequency and quality were improved by the Council. The result has been an increasing number of activists who can build the Council and shape and promote policy.

The Council has somewhat neutralized the influence of the Regional Director and staff. The staff member who coordinates bargaining no longer chairs the bargaining committee. As well, the Council provides a forum with clout to criticize or make proposals about staff. The OCHU also has a say in the selection of hospital sector staff coordinators.

The effect of these measures was to increase the rank and file's interest in the Council. One indication of this is the voluntary and very stable membership in the Council.

Hospital Workers in *CUPE*

As we noted earlier, hospital workers had not fared well in CUPE before 1981. There were residual prejudices due to the high composition of women workers, the historical employee characteristics, and the fact there had been no right to strike. Other CUPE members viewed hospital workers as complainers with little ability to act. The fact that there had been a strike of such magnitude changed many of these attitudes. The president of OCHU commented:

> I think perceptions are changed. The hospital workers themselves
> feel a pride in what they have accomplished. I think other CUPE
> members have a new respect as well. It's not something you can
> measure but you can feel it. (Interview, Barry, 1986)

Since the formation of OCHU there have been major shifts of responsibility. At the annual conference of the HCWCC in 1981, a senior
elected negotiator noted the lack of public relations and other support
from the Ontario Division leadership. At the same conference members from CUPE Local 79 (Riverdale Hospital) said:

> The leadership of this union must learn to look around them and to
> recognize the hospital workers and their needs or we will replace
> them. (Minutes of 1981 H.C.W. Conference, May 19–20, Windsor)

Since the creation of the OCHU, the criticisms of the Ontario Division
have been less frequent and the Ontario Division leader and executive have been pushed into relief.

The Health Care Workers Coordinating Committee (HCWCC) was
originally created as an organization of the Ontario CUPE Division.
OCHU took on all the coordination and communication functions
formerly handled by the HCWCC. This effectively severed most of the
day-to-day ties between the Ontario Division of CUPE and the hospital workers. Since the OCHU was founded, the HCWCC's primary
role has been the education of its members. This has been carried out
in coordination with the Council. The Council has good working relations with the CUPE National Executive Board (Barry Interview, 1986)
and with the departments at the national level (Levine Interview,
1986).

These developments are all positive for the union. There has finally
developed a respected place for hospital workers in CUPE.

Bargaining

Bargaining is a central activity for any trade union. Legislation
makes the union a legal bargaining agent. Along with enforcing
agreements, the major activity of a union is, in a legal sense, bargaining. Most issues are attached to bargaining. The OCHU functions
somewhat as a province-wide local of a union. However, it has no
legal standing in Ontario labour law. The Council is not a certified
bargaining agent. For that matter neither is the OHA. The constituent
members must voluntarily agree to bargain through their central bargaining structure before each round. They may opt not to be in-

volved. However, the relative success of the pseudo-central bargaining makes this difficult.

Bargaining through the Council is two-tiered. From the beginning, the central "table" had always shifted different issues to the local "tables." This circumvented problems of superior benefits and sticky local issues. For those locals that opt out of provincial bargaining, every issue is on their local "table." However, if they opt out they can end up accepting a contract that is less than what is anticipated in central negotiations. The hospital that is bargaining with a local that has opted out is kept informed by the OHA on developments at the central "table" to ensure that it does not offer items that are not being given at the central negotiations. Thus, in practice, there is little advantage to opting out. This pressure on locals to opt in reinforces the central system.

A review of bargaining since the Council was formed indicates some improvements:

1. In 1984 it succeeded in standardizing contract language and format among hospitals.

2. The superior benefits issue was partially solved by taking steps to sample existing agreements, which were put into a computer data base. If an issue was being discussed at the central table and a local had contract language that was superior, then the bargaining committee phoned to check the importance of the clause and sought agreement to bargain around it.

3. During this period the first "freely negotiated" settlement was achieved.

4. Membership participation and interest in bargaining has greatly increased since OCHU's formation.

THE CHANGES FOR WOMEN

Women and the OCHU

The Council's leadership wanted, according to the recollections of some of the leaders, to enhance the role of women in the union. In this study we can point three general areas to assess the status of women in the union and their role and relationship to the union. These are: (1) style of work and special measures within the union, (2) women in elected positions, and (3) the relevance of union actions, such as bargaining, to women.

Style of Work and Organization

Senior hospital workers comment that it is often the case that "women have no history of talking or speaking out." For this reason, the OCHU executive introduced a system of flexible parliamentary procedure. The establishment of clear rules of procedure makes it possible to learn how to participate. Indeed, the Council trained rank and file members on how to use these procedures. The flexibility mentioned above involved innovative application of the rules in order to allow less aggressive delegates to get to the floor to speak. This flexibility includes recognizing first-time speakers before repeat speakers and soliciting views of delegates who are knowledgeable, even if they are not in front of the microphone.

> Your first convention can be frightening. You don't really know if your idea fits in or if you can explain it properly. Unless you get helped a bit you can't really get up to do it. I remember being asked by the president to get up. They did not rush me. I haven't stopped talking out since! (RNA, first time delegate to 1984 Convention)

> I told them that I had been left standing at the mike [microphone] twice. The next time I got the nerve to stand up. I was way back in line and they asked me to step up ahead of others. (Dietary Worker)

The special measures necessary to get women more active are not restricted to the floor of the convention. To get more women to run for delegate positions, the critical issue of family and union responsibilities had to be addressed. One central aspect was child care. The existence of quality child care at conventions is important. President Barry noted in an interview:

> We found that very few were using the facilities but we kept it up anyway. We identified several problems. I think the thought of having kids come to a two or three day convention was too much. The sessions often go too long and we have night sessions too. Parents felt it was too long for kids to be in the daycare. One measure we took was to subsidize home daycare. (Paul Barry, Interview, 1986)

As we pointed out before, the under-utilization of the daycare is deceptive. If women know there is quality child care, even if they decide not to use it, there is more likelihood they will put themselves forward as delegates for a convention. So the *existence* of the service is important even if it is not used. The move to subsidizing home based care, as explained by Barry, was an interesting alternative.

Women and Elected Positions

It is too early to tell whether the steps taken to increase the involvement of women will bear fruit on a permanent basis. There are *indications* that improvements have begun. By 1984 the over-representation of males on the executive had been corrected, and the female majority was maintained in 1985. There is still a gap between the average percentage of women in the hospitals (approximately seventy percent) and their representation in the OCHU executive, but this gap has narrowed since the strike. (The exact male/female composition of the hospital sector is not available.)

A shift was also evident in the composition of the Presidents of locals. While data is difficult to obtain, the 1978 percentage of women hospital presidents was 44%. By 1986, 64% of all presidents were women.[1] At CUPE's National Executive Board level women officers have not exceeded 25% of total numbers. This is not representative of the numbers of women in CUPE.

This male/female imbalance is reflected in most areas of CUPE. Only 30% of the Provincial Division leaders are women. There is only one woman at the senior Director or Assistant Director level and, of the 177 field staff, only 22 or 12.4% are female. The movement in OCHU to greater participation by women is evident, particularly in contrast to CUPE in general.

The Relevance of Bargaining to Women

The third major area to consider is around bargaining. Too often issues directly concerning women are dropped as negotiations progress. If bargaining is seen to serve women's interests inadequately, then they will not participate.

The Council has only bargained for a short period to date. The 1982 round was "scrubbed" due to legislated guideline settlements. The following round was negotiated and the third and most recent round went to arbitration. In 1986, the union put forward seven issues to the arbitrator. These included maternity leave, wages/pay

---

[1] Data was collected from reviews of membership and delegate lists at conventions. The sex of the delegates was determined by the first name and a verbal check with senior unionists who were present at the meetings. The possibility of error is small but does exist and would underestimate the increased participation of women.

Table 5.3: Gender Composition of the OCHU Executive

1982	6 male	3 female
1984	3 male	6 female
1985	4 male	5 female

SOURCES: Convention Delegate Lists; OCHU Mailing Lists

Table 5.4: Percentage of Female Membership in CUPE

Year	% of Female Members
1971	33.6%
1975	39.8%
1979	45.4%
1982	46.9%
1989 (est.)	48.9%

SOURCE: CUPE National Research Department

equity, vacations, job security, part-time protection, sick leave, disability and benefits. While all the issues affect women as hospital workers, several are primarily women's issues. Pay equity, maternity leave and protection for part-time workers have a more significant effect on women than on men. The union did not merely push the issues on the table. It actively campaigned around these issues. Pay equity, for example, was the subject of several internal communications and a set of innovative proposals to management. OCHU had campaigned with its members to get a ten dollar per hour minimum wage proposal, for males and females, accepted as the bargaining position. Table 5.5 shows the typical relationship between male and female wages in one occupation.

In its own words, the "central bargaining committee (CBC) was unable to make any progress with the hospitals on [the] $10 minimum wage proposal" (CUPE Bargaining Update, 1986: 1). In response to the intransigence, the CBC put forward an innovative proposal that would soften the costs of moving to pay equity by making the

Table 5.5: Comparison of Hourly Wages Between Male and Female Cleaning Staff in Selected Hospitals, 1985

Hospital	Female	Male
Chedoke/McMaster	9.28	9.96
St. Josephs (Guelph)	9.02	9.66
Humber Memorial (Toronto)	8.79	9.96
North Bay Civic (North Bay)	9.06	9.99

SOURCE: CUPE Research Department: selected hospital contracts.

classifications negotiable and stretching the funding commitments over a longer time. In the CBC's words:

> We have proposed the hospitals set up a provincial Pay Equity fund with 1% of their total compensation costs (about $2.67 million) and then sit down and negotiate with OCHU which female dominated jobs would receive pay equity upgradings. (CUPE, 1986)

A second major bargaining issue of relevance to women in this bargaining round was maternity leave. It is an issue that pertains to women and addresses the conflicts between home/family and work. The Council promoted the issue to its members through a series of pamphlets and kept the issue at the forefront to the final stages of bargaining. These "Bargaining '85" pamphlets had two purposes. They educated the public and demonstrated to arbitrators that the issue was important to the union. They also educated the union membership on the importance of the issue.

The arbitration process in 1985 was only partially successful. The arbitration was, once again, a "centre ground" or "split the difference" settlement. The award was "...sprinkled with phrases like 'having weighed the competing interests' and 'the exercise we undertake is one of balancing a number of factors' or '...better balancing of interests...'" (CUPE 1986: 1).

In the Burkett arbitration award, maternity leave was improved substantially but pay equity was ignored. The union had requested the employer pay maternity leave benefits on top of the unemployment insurance. This would bring payment levels during leaves to 75% of regular pay. The arbitrators, however, ignored the 17 week proposal of the union and imposed a two-week qualifying period. The union nominee to the arbitration board noted that "...there is no justification for a two-week waiting period, because the very purpose of the supplement is to recognize that women ought not be penalized for being the gender to bear children" (CUPE 1986: 2).

The original version of the new pay equity legislation, subsequently brought into force on January 1, 1988, did not cover hospital workers. Public sector workers not directly working for the state were to wait for a second bill. This changed at the last draft when public and private sectors were integrated into the new legislation. CUPE pushed for equity at the bargaining table, but the message in the arbitration award was clear: Wait for the government! There was no movement on the question.

In this round of negotiations, the union did not drop the women's issues. It is clear where the union stood. However, several interviewees made traditional criticisms of the union's actions in negotiations. A maintenance worker commented:

> What's the union doing messing with family questions. We should have left out all these extra type issues and gone for more basic stuff like money. Don't get me wrong, the union has to stand up for everyone—women too. But that leave for maternity cost all of us money.

> The maternity benefits now that's nice but not for everyone—we got to concentrate on issues that affect everyone, not just young gals who got husbands for money anyway. (Dietary Worker)

In the midst of these types of pressures, the union maintained its new balance of demands. The Council's adherence to this new philosophy can be attibuted, in part, to the people in key positions. Barry was sensitive to women's issues and the new staff appointment, Julie Griffin (now Julie Davis, secretary-treasurer of the Ontario Federation of Labour) was committed to pressing for women's rights as well.

Lastly, there are the moves to make the bargaining process more open to members. The executive held an arbitration review conference to accomplish this. The aim was to give members a chance to understand the award and to criticise and comment on the events leading to it.

In short, there has been an attempt by the union to make bargaining relevant to the women members at the local level.

The Effect on Women as Individuals

The involvement in a strike as extensive as this has many subtle effects on the participants. The relationship between people and events and the nature of both is in constant flux and change. There can be slow evolutionary change that belies observation or rapid, abrupt, and observable change. The strike was an event which prompted rapid change for women. The changes were both internal to themselves and involved their relationships with work and co-workers.

> I don't regret it—in fact I'm glad we struck. You couldn't begin to understand what it meant for me. I'm a different person at home and at work.

The reason a strike can facilitate such changes is because our experiences influence or create our ideas and understandings. Many researchers have noted that the isolation of the home can particularize women's vision of the world (see Porter 1983: 172–190). For example, inflation and underemployment are understood through experiencing their affect on the family budget. This gives the woman a particular view of economic reality. Work experiences also affect and help to shape world views (consciousness). It forces people to humble themselves or tax their limits. The daily human intercourse floods the senses and forces an expansion of our thinking. The massive disruption a person experiences in a strike calls into question many ideas and understandings. As Darcy has commented, the strike experience "...is liberating in its own right" as it challenges the often felt "...sense of powerlessness and dependency" women feel because of their relative lack of participation in out-of-home affairs (Darcy 1983).

In the 1981 hospital strike women noted three areas of change in consciousness/understanding/ideology. The first level was self-confidence. The strike, at the local levels, fell into the laps of ordinary workers. CUPE was unable to provide much support. Taking up this challenge women gained a new confidence:

> I'd 've never thought I would do it. You surprise yourself when times like this come up. Now I'm much more confident about my ideas and everything. (Clerk, Interview, Hamilton)

This was reflected in home relations for some:

> I told my husband that I was right a lot more than he realized. If I had been able to make strike decisions, I was able to make house decisions. (Dietary worker, Interview, Hamilton)

Before the strike many women didn't see the union as theirs. After the strike there was a closer identification:

> My question was silly. Who the heck had run the union before the strike. I knew the answer and I wanted the chance to say we were going to do it together now. (Housekeeper, Interview, Hamilton)

> Once you know a bit about things you can help run the union. I didn't think I could do anything before. I guess some of the union talk of "it's *your* union" is right. (RNA, Hamilton)

Second, women also noted their pride as workers was affected by the fact they had stood up and "saved face." Their pride was restored and many said they felt conditions would be much worse if it were not for the strike.

Third was women's understandings of the process, institutions, and structures that they were part of. Women received a taste of the role of law and the state.

> I use to see the Government as kind of like a ref [referee] in a game trying to stop people from killing each other. Now that's part of it but they also got their bias and their own wants. They went after us, no fairness there. (RNA, Hamilton)

> What can you say anymore—I couldn't tell the difference between the Government and the hospitals. I wonder who was paying who. (Laboratory Technician)

Defying the law and courts made those institutions seem much less omnipotent. The anger towards the Government for what was perceived as pro-management labour laws and enforcement was translated, for some workers, into militancy.

There was little evidence among the workers of a massive shift politically, but cynicism, hostility, and a re-evaluation of the Government was evident. In response to the question about whether they would defy the law and strike again, many workers responded affirmatively. The vast majority said that, under the right conditions and with proper support and preparation, they might strike again. Many experienced a leap in thinking also. The notion of political struggle was part of many people's thinking (if they thought change was to be pursued):

> Go on strike—maybe but I'll tell you the only way we're going to get our rights is to push the Government to change the law. If that means marching on Queen's Park or changing governments so be it. (Dietary Worker)

> Maybe other tactics are better you know like protests or disobedi-
> ence—things like that. It's the law that's got to change. (Laboratory
> Technician)

Other changes related to the home and a woman's relation to it.
The different life and family situations of workers influenced the nature of these changes. For single women, involvement in the strike
process built confidence. Some of these women had to fight with
boyfriends over the strike and to deal with family and friends who
cautioned against action.

> They all said I should use my head and not get involved. My father,
> my boyfriend, they sounded the same. I made two big decisions,
> first I decided to ignore them, then I went ahead with the strike.

> It was a necessity, it brought us back to life, it restored my pride.
> (Dietary Worker)

One young woman crossed the picket line as her husband watched
and told her what to do. Two hours later, in tears, she burst from the
building:

> I couldn't, I couldn't—all my friends, my God and me—yeah me. I
> wanted to strike. When I realized that I left to join my side... My
> husband is a good man but he doesn't think I understand what I'm
> doing. I can tell you things are so much better now. I put *my* ideas
> up now and make him listen. (Clerical Worker)

> It nearly destroyed us—he sayin no, me sayin I had to. I should say
> we're together still and the strike saved us. It made me wake up. I
> can decide things, big things, bigger things than I dreamed about.
> (Dietary Worker)

Many women reported increases in self-confidence, self-esteem, and
spousal respect.

These effects of the strike on women reinforce the discussion in
Chapter 3. While the women hospital workers were interested in both
intrinsic and extrinsic rewards from their paid labour, it was the
changes in the labour process and work environment that precipitated support for the strike. The strike gave workers some of the
rewards they sought from their paid work. This partially explains to
this day the positive attitude women have toward the ill-fated strike.

THE RIGHT-TO-STRIKE: THE HLDAA AND
COMPULSORY ARBITRATION

At its 1979 convention, CUPE delegates decided to campaign for the right to strike. The CUPE National Executive may not have taken this too seriously but the membership of CUPE seems to have. The hospital strike may have been the greatest test of the campaign. The lack of a genuine fight to forward the rights of hospital workers doomed the 1979 decision.

The HLDAA is still in place and unamended. The government clearly rebuffed any amendments that could weaken the *Act*. The government was also clear that the method for seeking change, i.e. the illegal strike, was unacceptable. The jailing of three union leaders was designed explicitly to make that statement. That statement was a warning that the government was in control and would not budge on demands presented outside sanctioned avenues.

The sanctioned avenues were trails well known to the union and unsuccessful to date.

6

Conclusions

In the wake of the 1981 CUPE hospital walk out, there were those who claimed it was an odd or exceptional act with little or no explanation. The results of our investigation suggest otherwise.

The 1981 hospital strike is an understandable occurrence resulting from a complex set of circumstances. It was partly caused by a deepening fiscal crisis that prompted the government to tighten expenditures and control labour. The tightening of government expenditures pressured hospital administrations to push for cost efficiency and increased labour productivity. The denial of the right to strike gave management a freer hand in trying to accomplish its goals. The "illegal" strike was the one method unionists considered available to them to deal with the problem.

One of the sets of measures introduced by the hospital management involved changes in the labour process. Women reacted to these changes because they seriously eroded the rewards they sought from work. Most women wanted things to go back to the way they had been. Men were also affected, but for a complex of reasons sought to be compensated for the changes. They feared more "take aways" in the future and hoped the strike might slow that down. The differences between men and women revolved around their different reward structures.

The RNAs were being replaced by the RNs and their bedside duties were being reduced. Patients were being moved out of the hospitals more quickly than in the past. The patient "turn-around time" was being reduced. Patients were literally being forced to do their convalescing at home, so that the workers did not see and communicate with patients during the most positive recovery stages. Patients were, on average, more acutely ill. The work became more difficult, the interaction with patients decreased, and the sense of accomplishment in terms of health-care delivery was diminished. This led the

RNAs to assess their health-care standards as dropping. The introduction of split shifts and the use of part-time and on-call persons aggravated this.

The housekeepers reported having had an attachment to *their* ward and *their* patients. They had pride, knew the nurses and regulars. The housekeeper saw herself as part of the health-care team. In the mid- to late-1970s this changed. Budget-cutting measures led to changes in the location of work. The hospitals gave the housekeepers multiple wards, moving them every few days; shifts were altered and the pace of work quickened. Housekeepers felt that the standards of cleanliness and disease control were being reduced. Full-time housekeepers saw an increasing use of part-time and "on-call" persons and their own hours may even have changed. The pride was gone, the work done was not of the same quality because the pace was faster, and there was less attachment to a job well done. There was a separation from the rewarding, care-giving aspects of work such as the "chatting up" of patients. This, reported interviewees, was frustrating.

Dietary workers were separated from any contact with patients. The preoccupation with productivity improvement through further consolidation of assembly line techniques was distressing and led to a further separation from the job (for a discussion of this alienation from work, see Rinehart 1986: Chapter Two).

The laboratory technologists reported that the rate and volume of tests coming to them increased rapidly and the status of the tests changed. More and more tests arrived "stat" (emergency or priority) and this put pressure on the technologist. The laboratory technicians found themselves doing work on a mix of testing equipment at unfamiliar rates. This was not well received by the technologists who saw their work as an important aspect of the health-care delivery system. They worried about how sloppy or rushed work might affect the patient and other health-care workers.

Why did these changes provoke a strike? We suggested that there was a continuum between home and the paid workplace. For women, the work in the home was expressed as the transformation of resources into services for the family. This was work that could be unfulfilling. Service work in the hospital was on the continuum between home and paid labour. The service work in and of itself was not the sufficient condition for women choosing work in the hospital. There was a complex of rewards, including formal *recognition* of the usefulness of the work, an *interaction* with other workers, and an intrinsic *sense of a job well done.* The hospital work provided this complex of rewards. Care-giving was a key aspect of this. Labour process changes broke this care-giving bond for many women workers. The desire to reestablish this bond was one consideration in the decision to strike.

Men responded to their changing situation as well. Increases in compensation, a reduction in workload, and protection of benefits, (such as the sick leave plan) were the male unionists' goals in the strike. The male unionists were concentrated in work areas with less patient contact and a much reduced care-giving component. This was a non-service, non-care giving milieu that reinforced the reward system of the men. The search for compensatory, extrinsic rewards for changes in the workplace characterized the men of the hospital.

Caution must be exercised in applying this male-female/extrinsic/intrinsic division outside the hospital sector. However, in workplaces that have a care-giving component, the gender specific responses of workers helps to explain many things. In the case of the 1987 hospital workers' strike in Ontario, the different reward system was crucial.

The economic and political situation in Ontario also played a significant role in creating the conditions for the strike. The increasing fiscal problems forced the state to take restraint measures. The costs for health care were predicted to escalate rapidly. The federal government passed the responsibility for cost control to the provinces. The provinces in turn made dollars more scarce and forced hospital administrations to take a series of actions, including cutting staff, initiating productivity enhancement policies, changing work organization, and replacing full-time workers with part-time workers. The government also embarked on a set of labour restraint policies. These included wage controls, the retention of seriously flawed compulsory arbitration, and the ban on strikes (despite the growing evidence of serious flaws with such a ban).

These policies weakened the union, severely distorted bargaining, and subverted democracy. Because traditional channels, such as free collective bargaining, were no longer effective due to the labour restraint legislation, the only option for many workers was to go on strike.

The union's organization, structure, and functioning also affected the decision to strike. Rank and file workers had few "windows" on the decision-making process. CUPE's practice of hiring staff at the national level, and directing their work centrally, made it impossible for locally-elected people to direct the work of the staff. The disagreement between some local leaders and the staff over whether to strike raised democratic issues in many workers' minds. They saw the staff who were in charge of negotiations as outsiders subverting their interests. This contributed to the overwhelming vote to strike. Part of the vote was *against* the perceived manipulation by the staff and central union. This problem was aggravated by the infighting amongst staff and the union's upper level officers. That these factors contributed to a confrontation with management was confirmed by the interviewees in this study.

The structuring of union work discourages women from participating. There are many different types of time problems that are gender specific. These time constraints face *any* women wanting to participate in *any* activity in addition to their regular work. This problem was compounded by the barriers to women's participation in the union.

The strike was thus partly caused by weaknesses in union organization and it precipitated major union reorganization. The restructuring accomplished several things. An intermediate body was formed that was responsible to the union membership. This has strengthened elected hospital union officials vis à vis staff and created a forum for dealing with the problems of democracy. The union has also introduced internal changes that encourage more active involvement by women.

GENDER, RESISTANCE AND ACTIONS OF THE STATE

We set out in the beginning to discuss the causes and effects of the strike. We also wanted to use the case study to look at Braverman's research and his conclusions. We did not explore the deskilling and scientific management aspects of the Braverman thesis. The three areas of criticism that we explored were (1) Braverman's underestimation of the resistance of workers to labour process changes; (2) his blind spot to gender in the context of the labour process and the effect of the linkages between home and paid labour; and, (3) his downplaying of the role of political environment and fiscal crisis in labour process changes.

In our study, we found that both men and women opposed or disliked changes in their working conditions (i.e., workloading, changing duties, change of work locations, etc.). While some unionists opposed the strike, and there were some staff and senior elected officers who were accommodating to management when it made these types of changes, much of Braverman's thinking seems to rest on an assumption that unionists will accept and promote changes initiated by management, i.e. act as "an aristocracy of labour." John Goldthorpe's studies of carworkers in Britain echo a similar theme: the "affluent worker model" will accept dollars in return for dropping their resistance to labour process change. In the 1981 Ontario hospital strike this was simply not true. Unionists swept past the leadership group that wished to stop the strike. They demonstrated resistance where wages were not the articulated issue and where more intrinsic rewards were important. Braverman's view downplays the potential of working people to influence their working lives.

Braverman also avoided or ignored the interrelationship of women's role in home and in the paid labour processes. Our study suggests that the complex relation between home and paid labour helped to generate resistance to the changes outlined above. Women sought employment to fulfill several needs. The foremost was financial but this was not the sole, nor sufficient reason, for entering the paid work force. Women workers brought with them certain feelings, ideas, and wants that were conditioned by their experiences in family settings. As noted above, a complex of rewards was sought that family life had not satisfied. When the service/care links, interpersonal relations, and pace and method of work were altered by management, there was a deep disappointment, resentment, and finally resistance. The desire to reestablish the original labour process contributed to the decision to strike. Braverman's blind spot to gender is serious. His view of women is rooted in the sphere of consumption and he restricts his discussions to this domain. By ignoring gender, he ignores a source of potential worker resistance.

There is a third problem with Braverman's appraisal of labour process change. Our study underlines the importance of fiscal policy and the legal environment in shaping industrial relations. The decisions to alter the labour process by introducing part-time workers, changing the location of work, changing the pace and content of work, and eliminating male cleaners and orderlies were prompted by the budgetary pressures to increase productivity. New conditions of work were enforced by *legislative* restrictions on the right to strike and the arbitration process. Our study suggest that, particularly in the public sector, the economic and political circumstances are of great importance in understanding the labour process and reactions by workers to changes in their working conditions. Braverman makes the error of not exploring the potential differences between the private industrial setting and the public sector. This, in turn, leads him to gloss over state policies that affect the general conditions of work and worker-management relations.

THEORIES OF STRIKES

Popular explanations of the strike are rooted in the agency of the participants. It is claimed that the strikes are fomented by the agitators, leftists, or misleaders. Popular theories offer no explanation of *why* people strike. They are simply led to it, victims of a force external to their own decision making. As Hyman (1972: 57–8) notes, this is not a sociological analysis since it ignores the fact that people must have grievances in order to be motivated to take militant action. Leaders are at best "instruments of conflict, not the actual cause." In the case of the 1981 hospital strike the "agitator-misleader" explanation belittles the role of women and the understanding women have of their decisions. It portrays most women workers as dupes of a few male leaders. This was patently false in the 1981 hospital strike.

The assumption underlying popular theories is the equilibrium of society. However, the desire to find an aberrant reason for the conflict allows participants and outsiders to ignore the real causes of the strike. For example, the Government was not interested in examining its labour legislation or fiscal policies. This "structural-functional" bias is not limited to the popular theories. A review of strike theories in the scholarly field suggests a similar bias. Hyman divides the studies of strikes into two catagories (Hyman 1972: 56). The first is a variety of approaches similar to the structural-functionalist model. In such studies, evaluation of the causes and effects of strikes is implicitly or explicitly based on the examination of previous actions. The aim is to gather a list of characteristics which indicate a proneness to strike. For example, an examination of the social conditions surrounding a large number of Canadian strikes indicates that they will likely occur during periods of high inflation and are less likely to occur under conditions of high unemployment (Anderson 1982). This allows the social scientist to look at a set of circumstances and predict the potential for a strike, i.e. a strike is more likely under certain circumstances than others. There are two difficulties with this approach. First, while this approach may give an indication of the statistical proneness to strike, given a set of conditions, it does not *explain* why a strike happened. Second, the structure tends to become the only consideration under examination. People, or the actors of history, become passive in face of the sweep of structural determinants. The most advanced case of this is the various Dunlop-style "system analyses" (Dunlop 1956).

An alternate approach to explaining strikes—the one employed in our study—explores the particular event and ferrets out the causes and the rationale. This involves working at two levels of analysis. The researcher looks at both the structural determinants *and* the motivations (ideas, conceptions, and social consciousness) of the participants (Hyman, 1972: 56). In the cast of the 1981 Ontario hospital strike, we neither wish to say that the strike is unique (because motivations are unique), nor do we to say that the structure was totally determinant. Rather, we wish, in Hyman's words, to do an analysis where ... "social structure and social consciousness are dialectically related, each acting upon and influencing the other, and in some instances leading to increased stability and in others to heightened conflict" (Hyman 1972: 68).

The link between structure and agency is action. Action is not simply "called forth" by the structure. While structure encourages certain actions and circumscribes others, action is also dependent on how people assess the situation. The actions of individuals and groups stem from " ... the goals and motives which the participants bring with them" (ibid.). The structure of relations and the predispositions, motivations, and understandings that people have are interrelated related, with each influencing and being influenced by the other. For example, the law denying the right to strike discourages collective action but unionists may strike because there is a general disenchantment with the way labour relations develop with that law in place. Instead of the legal circumstances determining events, in practice the decisions of the workers are the important consideration.

These are not new ideas. They were originally developed by Marx (see Archibald 1985). In his political writings the notion of individuation and human agency are developed. In the famous phrase from the *Eighteenth Brumaire of Louis Bonaparte*, Marx comments: "men (sic) make their own history but not under conditions of their own choosing." Human beings set out to change the material world through work but find themselves changed in the course of this activity. The development of consciousness occurs as we live and work. "Being determines consciousness," argued Marx, or more properly: consciousness, attitudes, worldviews, or motivations come from somewhere and that "somewhere" is the living interaction with structures and people around us. This same consciousness propels people into actions and, as they act, they themselves condition the structures.

This approach demands that the researcher look at the personal and structural antecedents of the event to be explained. It encourages the researcher to seek explanation in the complex interconnections of production and reproduction. It encourages the researcher to deal with both the surface level and the deeper levels of explanation and description. This approach opens up important avenues of research. The structural determinants seemed to mitigate against a hospital strike in 1981, but the particularities of the union and the unionists led to a strike.

SOME IMPLICATIONS

There is much to be learned from a study of the public sector. The public sector differs from the private sector in several ways. The public sector worker is more vulnerable to political decisions than the private sector worker. The budgeting and planning process differ due to public demands and fiscal restraints. Industrial relations are different between the two sectors as well. The industrial relations differences are manifested in how the union may approach public management. Often the union, as in our study, appeals to the public at large in order to gain leverage against management. Management also appeals to the public as taxpayers in holding down costs.

An aspect of the public sector is its proximity and vulnerability to the political climate. This has a direct effect on unions in the public sector. In our study, we saw that the federal and provincial governments instituted wage controls which affected the incomes and working conditions of the hospital workers. Restrictive labour legislation (the HLDAA) was maintained despite mounting evidence in government studies indicating serious problems. The cost-cutting measures introduced at the federal level also affected the working lives of the hospital employee.

These political and economic circumstances, according to many of the hospital workers we interviewed, also affected those "consuming the service," i.e., the patient. Perhaps this concern of the workers stems from being able to directly see the consumption of the "product." The service/care link produced a desire for quality. The hospital workers in our study saw positive service being delivered as a reward of the job.

One can see that this relationship has many potential applications in industrial relations. Possibly unlike workers in the private sector, the public sector worker may resist changes to the work environment if feel they have a stake in the smooth and quality production of public service. More study is needed to assess these unique aspects of the labour process in the public sector.

This study is also important because it highlights the gender specific aspects of the changing labour process. Women and men reacted somewhat differently to the changing work environment of the hospital. The women interviewed in Hamilton/Burlington emphasized internal (intrinsic) rewards, whereas the men wished to protect monetary and fringe benefits. The explanation for this lies in the relationship between home and paid work, which was a second major theme of this study. Perhaps the implications of this view are most clearly seen in relation to union structure and action. The desire to expand female participation within the unions will partially depend on recognizing the limitations placed on women by their responsibilities in the home. There was and remains a dearth of material in this important area.

The last implication concerns the debate on the labour process in general. This case study in Hamilton-area hospitals suggests that many of the criticisms of Braverman are justified. The influences which Braverman ignored—gender, resistance, and political/fiscal environment—were particularly important in the hospital strike. More research into this area could also prove to be valuable in our efforts to understand the meaning of work.

APPENDIX 1

Methodology

Methodology is essentially the procedure used to understand or explain an event or phenomenon. One can investigate a phenomenon from several directions. One method is to set rigid hypotheses and, observing established statistical procedures, test these hypotheses. This demands that the data be gathered under strict rules and it requires a sample that can yield information relevant to the hypotheses being tested. While this method has its place in research, this study is in a different tradition. This is an exploratory case study, a widely-used form of sociological investigation. It focusses on the "event" to cast light on the wider complexities of structural and individual/group determination of action. The case study approach is flexible as Selltiz, Johoda, Deutsch and Cook (1959: 60) point out:

> What features of this approach make it an appropriate procedure for evolving insights? A major one is the attitude of the investigator which is one of receptivity, of seeking rather than testing. Instead of limiting himself to the testing of existing hypotheses, he is guided by the features of the object being studied. His inquiry is constantly in the process of reformulation and redirection as new information is obtained.

This study was conducted in this way—"seeking rather than testing." The role of women in the strike became clearer during the study and demanded a reformulation of some concepts previously accepted. It became clear that the women strikers had significant differences from the men. This was true in terms of motivation, the relation with the union, and the general relationship between women and their work. This had to be investigated. The case study approach allowed this change of direction.

The great quantity of data we collected ranged from general union policies to the daily thoughts and conversations of individuals. Vari-

ous ways of reanalyzing this information uncovered hidden or ob-
scured relationships between factors.

On the other hand, the case study format has several drawbacks. It
usually does not allow one to generalize the findings to other situations. The researcher must be content with claiming the findings
"suggest" certain relationships between actions or among the individuals studied. A second weakness concerns comparability. The flexibility that is inherent in the method implies that different studies
may have significant differences in approach, so that the basis for
comparing and contrasting studies is made more difficult or impossible. The third problem concerns the use of statistical techniques. The
data collected in the exploratory case study most often do not conform to the sampling rules and therefore do not allow one to carry
out many statistical manipulations.

Data Sources

The four sources for the data used in this study were: (1) Government documents/publications; (2) newspapers; (3) Archives and; (4)
Interviews.

Government Documents

Repeated studies have been done to evaluate labour legislation and
the overall effectiveness of the health care system. This provided a
wealth of information on the labour relations in the hospitals. Despite
the interest exhibited by the government, and the participants in the
system, there has been very little interest in the academic community.
Informative works from the 1971 commentary by Isbester to Kruger's
1985 evaluation of hospital industrial relations are exceptions to the
rule.

Newspapers

Newspapers are an often underrated source of valuable information for social research. We reviewed the print media for the period
just before, during and for several months after the strike. This was
carried through by new computer search techniques combined with
manual searches (The decade before the strike was not accessible elec-
tronically). Newspapers provided some management views, union
opinions and public perceptions. Newspapers were also used to fol-
low up leads. For example, during an interview, a contact mentioned
that she had been interviewed years earlier by a newspaper reporter

on the wage problems in the hospitals. Researching these earlier articles provided some informative data on wage problems and staff
turnover in the early 1970s. This eventually helped to explain strike
motivations.

Archival Materials

The four major archival sources for this study were: (a) Minutes of
meetings; (b) Union-management documents; (c) Union Publications
and; (d) Personal Correspondence.

This type of data is not found in filing cabinets alone. The approximately 5000 pages of material gathered were found in basements,
closets, attics, estates and even abandoned automobiles. The help of
union people in gathering material was remarkable. Hospital workers
and union officials "bent over backwards" to find materials such as
old leaflets, membership lists, strike reports and much more. Once
someone woke the author up during the night to pass over personal
notes from meetings that were over five years old. Archival material
is *very* important in two respects. The material is obviously data in
and of itself but it can be more. The material acts as a check on the
recollection of the participants. Interviews provided one view of the
happenings at meetings that took place five years earlier. People's
notes, and the official meeting minutes, can be used to verify the
accuracy of the interpretation given in the interviews. They may also
be consulted to determine biographical and personal characteristics.
For example, the number of female unionists at a convention or meeting can be assessed using sign-in sheets or expense vouchers.

Minutes are any form of material that record the events of a meeting. They can be the official record of the meeting or someone's personal notes on the event. Both types of minutes were used and the
two types provided a check on each other. The resulting information
told the story of some key periods. The "Rowhampton massacre"
(discussed in Chapter 4), for example, took on added meaning after
evaluating the various records. It is important to note that individuals
attending these types of gatherings tend to take personal notes and
many keep these records (but did not file them).

Documents that pass between the union and management provide
a record of the industrial relations and shed light on the aspirations,
plans and failed enterprises of the participants. We examined the
collective agreements, memoranda of conditions to bargain, prepara-
tory research for bargaining, union submissions to bargaining, docu-

mentation around the arbitrations of agreements, bargaining reports and correspondence between the parties. These created a picture of the evolving interaction of the major players in the event we are investigating.

The third area of archival research was union publications. This included newsletters, magazines, journals, bargaining updates and information bulletins. These helped to place issues in a wider context.

The last archival source used was personal correspondence. The researcher had access to many letters written to the union staff and officials from union members. These provided a perspective on how the rank and file saw the actions being taken and helped us verify the interview data. The debacle around the appointment of the hospital coordinator (discussed in Chapter 4) came alive in the critical letters sent to CUPE's leaders. The members made their displeasure with the choice for coordinator clear. There were some accidental finds that were also of interest. The correspondence between the administrator of a large public general hospital and the Mayor of Hamilton gave our research its only accurate assessment of the danger facing patients during the hospital strike.

Interviews

There are several types of interviews, including the focused or structured interview, the semi-structured interview and the open interview. Each interview method has its advantages and disadvantages. The focused interview allows each of the interviews to be compared because the questions, the content of presentation etc. are identical. The interviews are similar to extended questionnaires although, as Merton argues, "the manner in which the questions are asked and their timing [can be] largely left to the interviewers discretion" (Merton 1958). These types of interviews are important in gathering data for statistical manipulations.

With the open interview, on the other hand, there is no predetermination of the exact questions or the range of response permitted (see Sellitz, et. al. 1959: 262–63). This approach allows the discovery of hitherto unimagined relationships. The persons being interviewed are allowed full input in defining the subject of the interview. The difficulty posed by this method is comparability. The non-focused nature of the interviews means they differ and therefore responses can not be easily compared.

The semi-structured interview is a cross between the two other formats. It uses the same set of questions in each interview but these are open ended and can be followed up with supplementary questions when the interview seems to warrant this approach. This form of interview was employed in our study.

The respondents for the interview were selected from the Hamilton-Burlington area. The case study is restricted to this area in terms of rank and file workers. The upper echelons of the union, the Ontario Hospital Association (OHA) and government officials interviewed were located in different areas of the province. Hamilton-Burlington was selected because it was a "typical" area in some ways. The mix of characteristics in the hospitals available for study made it a representative centre. It is a major urban centre and most hospital workers are located in such centres. It was possible to select hospitals that parallelled both the various types of institutions that exist in the province (i.e. chronic versus acute) and the differing involvements in the strike. It was an active strike location, as were Ottawa and Sudbury. Some of its hospitals were only peripherally involved (such as Joseph Brant) while one hospital walked out on a wildcat strike days before the rest of the province (St. Peters). Although each hospital is a separate entity with its own history, the budgeting and organization are similar across the urban areas of Ontario. Therefore many structural factors are the same across the province. Even so, the case study can only suggest certain things about the province as a whole. In choosing hospitals we tried to approximate the range of hospitals that existed province-wide. This meant interviewing in chronic care, public acute care institutions, general hospitals, and smaller regional ones. Hospitals that were very active in the strike and hospitals that did not stay out on strike were also selected.

The selection of interviewees was also important. Very different types of work exist within the workplace and these were thought to be important in the causation of the strike. Therefore, persons from different types of work were interviewed. We divided the hospitals into five major departments: housekeeping, foodservices, nursing, maintenance and the laboratories. We interviewed two persons from the clerical area but did not pursue a systematic investigation of this work area due to difficulties securing a sample. Where feasible a representative male-female "sample" was interviewed in each department. We interviewed a range of respondents across the various cate-

Table A.1: Interviewees by Department and Gender

Department	Male	Female	Total
Housekeeping	2	8	10
Dietary (foodservices)	3	5	8
Nursing	2 (porter/orderly)	9	11
Maintenance	4	0	4
Laboratory	2	3	5
Clerical	0	2	2
Total	13	27	40

gories (i.e. age, marital status, etc.) but the investigator did not rely on the sample being proportional in the strictest sense of the word.

The three distinct categories among the interviewees were: (1) key informants (i.e. individuals at the local or central level of CUPE with an insight into the events surrounding the strike); (2) general informants, (i.e. the rank and file hospital workers); and, (3) hospital, police and government officials.

The key informants were usually activists who supported or opposed the strike. General informants included men and women who opposed and supported the action. Supporters of the action were deemed to be those who voted for the strike. This was the vast majority of the union members. The other category of general informants were the members involved in the suspensions and firings. It was difficult to find people who opposed the strike from beginning to end. There are only three in the sample. Interestingly, the interviews do not significantly change across this support/non support difference. The unionists who did *not* support the strike did so because they felt it would not succeed or because spousal pressures made support impossible. They agreed with the strikers with regards to the problems in the workplace and in collective bargaining.

The breakdown of the interviews is shown in Table A.1. The interviewees were distributed across the 6 regional hospitals in this proportion: Hamilton General 13; Hamilton Henderson 11; St. Josephs 4; St. Peters 5; Chedoke 3; and Joseph Brant (Burlington) 4. In addition, interviews were conducted with two government officials, eight senior union officers, three senior management personnel, two non-hospital workers active in support work, a past Mayor of Hamilton, two former police officers, a former Tory advisor and one person intimate with several arbitrations. There were, therefore, 61 interviews conducted in all. Potential interviewee's names were secured from key informants. We requested contacts who were supporters and non-supporters. Through cross-listing people by workplace, gender and described attitude the final list of possible interviewees was determined. The key informants were very accurate in their assessment of people. Where the informants were not accurate in their assessment replacements were sought out.

We first constructed an interview schedule that was used in the first round of interviews with the key informants. The questionnaire was revised in minor ways as a result of these interviews. The revisions were in the area of accuracy of presentation and phrasing. These changes had to do with organization of the work day. Several questions relating to previous employment were dropped as they were deemed of less import in the rather lengthy schedule. The author conducted the interviews himself. They ranged from one and one half hours in two cases to five hours in the case of Grace Hartman (Past President of CUPE). The interviewees were asked if the interviews could be taped. Only two people chose not to be taped but close to half of the interviewees explicitly demanded that no transcripts of their interviews be made. They did not want to be identified directly or indirectly in the text. We agreed that no transcripts would be made available to anyone other than the researcher and that quotes would be identified by real occupation/department but not by hospital. The interviewees felt it was too easy to narrow down the possible identities in any other format. Most of the interviewees were reluctant to be identified. The severe repercussions after the strike reminds people still that conflicts are "serious business" and one must be careful not to expose oneself to future consequences. Others felt their work in the union could be affected. Many others felt their opinions were their own and while they would share them with the researcher, they wanted anonymity.

The interviews were conducted in the homes of the people, or in difficult cases, after work over a drink. The process of getting through all the interviews was somewhat inefficient as the times were picked by the respondents. However the rewards were great when the interviewee picked the time and place. They were more comfortable and more willing to talk. The interviews were set up with the promise that one hour would be adequate but the interviewees themselves often wanted to continue longer. The process of gathering interview data went smoothly except for some small frustrations, such as missed meetings or late arrivals.

In retrospect the collection of data was long and difficult but quite exciting and ultimately extremely rewarding. Some difficulties should be pointed out. A lot of the interview based-data suffered from time lag. The distance from the strike meant that people had to reconstruct the event. The interview data must then be triangulated using other interviews and written records to verify comments. This was done. The quotes used here were *typical responses*. This is a central methodological point. What constituted "typical" vs "unique" was assessed carefully. Interviews were repeatedly reviewed to search for patterns of repeated issues and interpretations as well as for differences. Care was taken not to claim responses as typical if there was doubt about such a judgement.

The data were collected in a way that *allowed* this investigation to examine historically both the interrelation of events and the actions and feelings of the individuals involved.

Bibliography

The following Bibliography contains four sections. Section I documents secondary literature directly pertinent to the analysis of the strike and its participants. Section II is a record of the newspapers consulted from 1963 to 1986. Section III records the Government Documents related to this study. Section IV is the primary research material used. The record in Section IV is complex as it is a very abridged selection of the approximately five hundred documents generously turned over to the author by members of the Canadian Union of Public Employees. Only those documents that are referenced in the text and/or directly influenced the direction of the argument are reported. They are grouped by certain key identifiers, based on the type of document (correspondence, newsletter, etc.) and their date. Titles for unnamed documents are consistent with references in the text.

SECONDARY LITERATURE

Aaron, Benjamin; Joseph R. Grodin and James L. Stern. *Public-Sector Bargaining*. BNA Publishing, Washington, D.C., 1979.

Abrams. *Historical Sociology*, London, 1984.

Adams, G. "The Ontario Experience with Interest Arbitration" *Relations Industrielles*, Vol. 36, No. 1, 1981.

Anderson, J. "Determinants of Collective Bargaining Impasses" in *Conflict Management in Industrial Relations* (ed.), G. Bomers and Richard Paterson. Nichoff, 1981.

———"Local Union Participation": *Industrial Relations*, Vol. 17, No. 3, October 1978

———"Local Union Participation: a reappraisal," *Industrial Relations*, Vol. 18, No. 1, Winter 1981.

Anderson, J. and Morley Gunderson. *Union-Management Relations in Canada*. Toronto: Addison-Wesley, 1982.

Anderson, P. *Debates in English Marxism*. London: NLB, 1979.

Andreopoulos, Spyros. *National Health Insurance: Can We Learn From Canada?* John Wiley & Sons, New York, 1975.

Archibald, P. "Agency and Alienation: Marx's Theories of Individuation and History," *Studies in Political Economy*, No.16, Spring, 1985.

Armstrong, H. "The Labour Force and State Workers in Canada" in Panitch (ed.) *The Canadian State.* University of Toronto Press, Toronto 1977.

Armstrong, Pat. "Female Complaints: Women, Health and the State." Unpublished Paper, Montreal, 1986.

Armstrong, Pat and Hugh Armstrong. *The Double Ghetto, Canadian Women and Their Segregated Work.* McClelland and Stewart, 1984.

————*A Working Majority, What Women Must Do For Pay.* Canadian Advisory Council on the Status of Women, Ottawa, 1983.

————"More For the Money: Redefining and Intensifying Work in Canada." Unpublished Paper, Montreal, 1986.

Armstrong, Pat, Hugh Armstrong, Patricia Connelly and Angela Miles. *Feminist Marxism or Marxist Feminism: A Debate.* A Network Basic, Toronto, 1985.

Badgely, R. "Health Workers Strikes." *International Journal of Health Services*, Vol. 5, No. 1, 1975.

Balbo, L. "The Servicing Work of Women and the Capitalist State," *Political Power and Social Theory*, Vol. 3, 1982.

Barker, D. and S. Allen. *Dependence and Exploitation in Work and Marriage.* Longman, London, 1976.

Beechy, V. "Some Problems in the Analysis of Female Wage Labour in the Capitalist Mode of Production." *Capital and Class*, No. 3, Autumn, pp. 45–66, 1977.

Beechy, V. "On Patriarchy," *Feminist Review.* No. 3, pp. 66–82, 1979.

Bell, D. *The Coming of the Post Industrial Society.* Basic Books, New York, 1973.

Bird, M. and R. Fraser. *Commentaries on the Hall Report.* Ontario Economic Council, Toronto, 1981.

Blauner, R. *Alienation and Freedom.* University of Chicago, Chicago Press, 1964.

Bloom, D. "Is Arbitration Really Compatible with Bargaining." *Industrial Relations*, 20(Fall)

Boivin, Jean. "Collective Bargaining in the Public Sector: Some Propositions on the Cause of Public Employee Unrest" in Gunderson *Collective Bargaining in Essential and Public Service Sectors.* University of Toronto, Toronto, 1975.

Bomers, Gerard B.J. and Richard B. Peterson. *Conflict Management and Industrial Relations.* Kluwer-Nijhoff Publishing, Boston, 1982.

Borman, Kathryn M., Daisy Quarm, and Sarah Gideonse. *Women in the Workplace: Effects on Families.* Ablex Publishing, Norwood, New Jersey, 1984.

Braverman. H. *Labour and Monopoly Capital.* Monthly Review Press, New York, 1974.

Briskin, L. "Women's Challenge to Organized Labour," in Briskin and Yanz (ed.) *Union Sisters*, Women's Press, 1983.

————"Women and Unions in Canada: A Statistical Overview" in Briskin and Yanz (ed.) *Union Sisters*, Women's Press, 1983.

Brock, Jonathan. *Bargaining Beyond Impasse*. Joint Resolution of Public Sector Labor Disputes. Auburn House, Boston, 1982.

Brown, C.A. "Women Workers in the Health Service Industry," *International Journal of Health Services*, Vol. 5, No. 1, 1975.

Burawoy, M. *Manufacturing Consent*. University of Chicago Press, Chicago, 1979.

Burman, Sandra. *Fit Work For Women*. Croom Helm, London, Canberra, 1979.

Butler, R. "Estimating the Narcotic Effect of Public Sector Impasse Procedures." *Industrial and Labour Relations Review*. Vol. 35, No. 1, Oct. 1981.

Calvert, J. *Canada Incorporated*. Canadian Centre for Policy Alternatives. Toronto, 1985.

Canadian Labour. "N.U.P.E. Hoists Hospital Strike," May, 1963.

Carter, G. E. "Financing Health and Post-Secondary Education: A New and Complete Fiscal Arrangement." *Canadian Tax Journal*, Vol. XXV, No. 5, September, 1977.

Cavendish, R. *Women on the Line*. Routledge, London, 1982.

Chaison, G., P. Andrappan. "Characteristics of Female Union Officers in Canada." *Relation Industrielles*, Vol. 32, No. 4, 1982.

Christensen, Sandra. *Unions and the Public Interest, Collective Bargaining in the Government Sector*. The Fraser Institute, Vancouver, 1980.

Clawson. *Bureaucracy and the Labour Process*. Monthly Review Press, New York, 1980.

Clegg, H. "Legal Framework" in Clegg and Flanders *The System of Industrial Relations*, Oxford 1954.

Coombs, R. "Labour and monopoly capital," *New Left Review*, Vol. 107, January-February, pp. 79–96.

Coser, L. A. *The Functions of Social Conflict*. Kegan and Paul, London, 1956.

Courchene, T. et al. (ed.) *Which Way Ahead? Canada After Wage and Price Control*. Fraser Institute, Vancouver, 1977.

Crouch, Colin. *State and Economy in Contemporary Capitalism*. St. Martin's Press, New York, 1979.

Culyer, A.J. *Measuring Health: Lessons for Ontario*. University of Toronto Press, Toronto, 1978.

Cuneo, C. "Barriers to Union Organizing: Struggling Against Patriarchal Classes." Unpublished Paper, 1986(a).

————"Trade Union Organizing: Struggling Against Patriarchal Classes." Unpublished Paper, 1986(b).

Dahrendorf, R. *Class and Class Conflict in Industrial Society*. Stanford University Press, Stanford, 1959.

Darcy, J. "The Right to Strike" in *Union Sisters* (ed.) B. Briskin and C. Yanz. Women's Press 1983.

————Untitled Letter. *The Clarion*. February 1981, p. 5.

————"Hospital Workers Won." *The Clarion*, Toronto, February 1982.

Delmar, R. "Looking Again At Engels' *Origins of the Family*," in J. Mitcheland, A. Oakley, *The Rights and Wrongs of Women*. Harmondsworth, Penguin, 1984.

Denton, Margaret Anne. *Industrial Sectors and the Determinants of Earnings: Male-Female Differences*. Ph.D. Dissertation, McMaster University, 1984.

Deverell, J. "The Ontario Hospital Dispute 1980–81." *Studies in Political Economy*, 1982.

Dixon, K. Hamilton Civics Hospital Memorandum to Department Heads and C.U.P.E. Members - Threatened Strike by C.U.P.E., January 23, 1981.

Downie, B. "Collective Bargaining Under an Essential Services Disputes Commission" in *Conflict or Compromise, The Future of Public Sector Industrial Relations*. Institute for Research on Public Policy.

Dulein, R. *Working Union Management Relations: The Sociology of Industrial Relations*. Prentice Hall, Engelwood Cliffs, 1958.

Dunlop, J. *Industrial Relations Systems*. Holt, New York, 1958.

Dworkin, A.G. and Chavetz, T. "Marcro and Micro Process in the Emergence of Feminist Movements." *Western Sociological Review*, Vol. 14, No. 1, 1983.

Edwards, Gordon and Reich. *Segmented Work Divided Workers*. Cambridge Press, Cambridge, 1982.

Edwards, P.K. and H. Sullivan. *The Social Organization of Industrial Conflict: Control and Resistance in the Workplace*. Blackwell, Oxford, 1982.

Ehrenreich, B. and Ehrenreich, J. "Hospital Workers: A Case Study in the New Working Class." *Monthly Review* (24) No. 8, 1973.

Ehrenreich, John. *The Cultural Crisis of Modern Medicine*. Monthly Review Press, New York, 1978.

Elshtain, J. "In Grand Manner," *Women's Review of Books*. January 1987, pp. 13–14.

Edelson, M. "Breaking Down the Barriers." *Our Generation*, Vol. 15, No. 3, Fall 1982.

Engels, F. *The Origins of the Family, Private Property and the State*. London, Lawrence and Wishart, 1972.

Esland, G. and G. Salaman. *The Politics of Work and Occupations*. University of Toronto Press, Toronto, 1980.

Evans, R. G. "Health Care Costs and Expenditures in Canada." Paper for *International Conference on Health Costs and Expenditures*. Washington, June, 1975.

Farker, H.S. "Does Final Offer Arbitration Encourage Bargaining." *Proceedings of the Thirty-Third Annual Meeting* (ed. Barbara Dennis), Denver, September 5–7, 1980.

Feuille, P. "Final Offer Arbitration and the Chilling Effect," *Industrial Relations*, Vol. 14, No. 3, October 1975.

———"Selected Benefits and Costs of Compulsory Arbitration." *Industrial and Labour Relations Review*, Vol. 33, No. 1. (Oct. 1979).

Finch, Janet and Dulcie Groves. *A Labour of Love: Women, Work and Caring*. Routledge and Kegan Paul, 1983.

Foot, David K. *Public Employment and Compensation in Canada: Myths and Realities.* Butterworth, 1978.

Foot David K. *Public Employment in Canada: Statistical Series.* Butterworth, 1979.

Fox, Alan. *A Sociology of Work in Industry.* Collier-MacMillan, 1978.

Fox, Bonnie. *Hidden in the Household, Women's Domestic Labour Under Capitalism.* The Women's Press, Toronto, 1980.

Fraser, R.D. *Canadian Hospital Costs and Efficiency.* Economic Council of Canada, Ottawa, 1971.

Friedman, A. *Industry and Labour.* MacMillan, London, 1977.

Gallagher, D. and Kurt Wetzel. "The Saskatchewan Governments Internal Arrangements to Accommodate Collective Bargaining." Working Paper 79–02, College of Commerce, University of Saskatchewan, 1979.

Gannage, Charlene. *Double Day, Double Bind, Women Garment Workers.* The Women's Press, Toronto, 1986.

Giroux, Claudette. *The Role of Women in the Canadian Trade Union Movement.* School of Social Work, Carleton University, Ottawa, 1978.

Goldstein, J.P. *The Micro-Macro Dialectic, The Concept of a Marxian Microfoundation in Research in Political Economy.* J.A. Press Inc., 1981.

Goldthorpe, J. et al. *The Affluent Worker: Industrial Attitudes and Behaviour,* Cambridge: Cambridge University Press, 1968.

Gonick, C. *Inflation and Wage Controls,* Canadian Dimension, Winnipeg, 1976.

Government of Saskatchewan. *Department of Social Services. Briefing Notes -* Federal-Provincial Cost Sharing Conference, Regina, 1976.

Graham, H. "Providers, Negotiators and Mediators: Women as the Hidden Carers" in Lewin and Olesen, *Women Health and Healing.* Tavistock Publishing, London.

Grant, Judith E. *Women's Part-Time Employment and the Reserve Army of Labour: A Theoretical Refinement and An Exploratory Investigation.* Master of Arts Thesis, McMaster University, 1983.

Gray, S. "Sharing the Shop Floor." *Canadian Dimension,* 18(2), 1984.

Griffin, L., Joel Devine and Michael Wallace. "On the Economic and Political Determinants of Welfare Spending in Post-World War II Era." *Politics and Society* 12, No. 3 (1983).

Guberman, N. "Working, Mothering and Militancy: Women in the C.N.T.U." in Briskin and Yanz (ed.) *Union Sisters,* Women's Press, 1983.

Gunderson, M. *Economic Aspects of Interest Arbitration.* Ontario Economic Council Discussion Paper Series. Toronto, 1983.

———*Collective Bargaining in the Essential and Public Service Sectors.* University of Toronto Press, Toronto, 1975.

Hartman, G. "Women and the Unions" in *Women in the Canadian Mosaic.* Peter Martin, Toronto, 1976.

Hicks, J. *The Theory of Wages.* MacMillan, London, 1932.

Hughes, Edward. *Hospital Cost Containment Programs, A Policy Analysis.* Ballinger, Cambridge, 1978.

Huxley, C. "The State, Collective Bargaining and the Shape of Strikes in Canada." *Canadian Journal of Sociology*, Vol. 4, No. 3, Summer, 1979.

Hyman, R. *Strikes*. Fontana, London, 1971.

Isbester, F. and S. Castle. "Labour Relations in Ontario Hospitals." *Relations Industrielles*, Vol. 26, No. 2, 1970.

Jamieson, S. *Times of Trouble*. Queens Printer, Ottawa, 1971.

Johnston, D.C. "Public Interest Disputes and Compulsory Arbitration: A Case Study of Hospitals in Ontario," *Ottawa Law Review*, Vol. 7, 1976.

Kelly, J.E. *Scientific Management, Job Redesign and Work Performance*, New York, Academic Press, 1982.

Kochon, T. "Estimating the Narcotic Effect: Choosing Techniques that fit the problems." *Industrial and Labour Relations Review*, Vol. 35. No. 1, Oct. 1981.

Kruger, A. "Collective Bargaining in Ontario Public Hospitals." *Relations Industrielles*, Vol. 40, No. 1, 1985.

Langford, Tom. *Gender and Worker Resistance, An Analysis of Studies of Women and Men Factory Workers*. Unpublished Paper, McMaster University, 1985.

Lerner, G. *The Creation of Patriarchy*. New York, Oxford University Press, 1986.

Levin, D. and Shirley B. Goldenberg. "Public Sector Unionism in the U.S. and Canada." *Industrial Relations* Vol. 19, No. 3 (Fall 1980).

Lieberman, Myron. *Public-Sector Bargaining*. A Policy Reappraisal. Lexington Books. D.C. Heath, Lexington, 1980.

Lipset, S.M. *Union Democracy*. Free Press, Glencoe, 1956.

Littler, C.R. 'Understanding Taylorism', *British Journal of Sociology*, Vol. 29, No. 2, pp. 185–202, 1978.

Littler, Craig, R. *The Development of Labour Process in Capitalist Societies: A Comparative Analysis of Work Organisation in Britain, the U.S.A. and Japan*, Heinmann, London, 1982.

Littler, Craig, R., and Salaman, Graeme. *Class at Work*, Batsford, London, 1984.

Low-Beer, John R. *Protest and Participation*. Cambridge University Press, Cambridge, 1978.

Luxton, M. *More Than A Labour of Love*, Women's Press, Toronto, 1980.

MacFarlane, L. J. *The Right to Strike*. Pelican Books, Harmondsworth, 1981.

MacIntosh, M. "Reproduction and Patriarchy." *Capital and Class*, No. 2, 1977, pp. 119–127.

MacKenzie, G. "The political economy of the American working class," *British Journal of Sociology*, Vol. 28, No. 2, pp. 244–52.

Mackie, M. *Exploring Gender Relations*. Butterworth, Toronto, 1984.

Marchak, P. "Women Workers and White Collar Unions." *Canadian Review of Sociology and Anthropology*, 1972.

Marchak, P. "The Political Economy of Womens Work" in H. Maroney (ed.) *The Political Economy of Women*. Methuen, Toronto, 1987.

Maroney, H.J. "Feminism at Work" in B. Palmer (ed.) *The Character of Class Struggle*. Toronto, 1984.

Martin, J. "Predictors of Industrial Propensity to Strike," *Industrial and Labour Relations Review*, Vol. 39, No. 2, January 1986.

Marx, K. *Class Struggles in France 1848–1850*. International Publishers, New York, 1964.

———*The Economic and Philosophic Manuscripts*. New World, New York, 1964.

———*Capital*. International Publishers, New York, 1967.

———*The Eighteenth Brumaire of Louis Bonaparte*. International Publishers, New York, 1974.

———*The German Ideology*. New world, New York, 1974.

———*The Grundrisse*. Harmondsworth, Penguin, 1976.

Maslove, A. and G. Swimmer. *Wage Controls in Canada 1975–78*. The Institute for Research on Public Policy, Montreal, 1980.

McFarland, J. "Women and Unions: Help or Hindrance." Atlantis, 1979.

McMurtry, Attorney General Roy. *Statement: Hospital Workers Strike*. Attorney General's Department, Saturday, January 31, 1981.

Milkman, Ruth. *Women, Work and Protest*. A Century of U.S. Women's Labor History. Routledge and Kegan Paul, 1985.

Montero, G. *We Stood Together*. Lorimer, Toronto, 1979.

Monthly Review. *Technology, the Labor Process, and the Working Class*. Monthly Review Press, New York, 1976.

O'Connor, J. *The Fiscal Crisis of the State*. St. Martins Press, New York, 1973.

O'Keeffe, Patrick. *A Personal Statement in Rebuttal of Statements Made by some Members of the Central Bargaining Committee*. C.U.P.E. Health-Care Workers Conference, May 1981.

Ontario Economic Council. *Issues and Alternatives Update*, Toronto, 1979.

Ontario Waffle. *The Struggle of Ontario Hospital Workers*. p. 537–551. n.d.

Panitch, L. (ed.) *The Canadian State*. University of Toronto Press, Toronto, 1977.

Panitch, L. and Don Swartz. "From Free Collective Bargaining to Permanent Exceptionalism: The Economic Crisis and the Transformation of Industrial Relations in Canada" in *Conflict or Compromise: The Future of Public Sector Industrial Relations*. Institute for Research on Public Policy.

Pathy, Alexander C. (ed.) *The Problem of "Essential Services": Inconvenience, Importance or Emergency*. Proceedings 17th Annual Conference of the McGill Industrial Relations Centre, 1979.

Penn, R. "Skilled Manual Workers in the Labour Process" in Wood, S. (ed.) *The Degradation of Work*. Hutcheson, London, 1982.

Penn, Roger. *Skilled Workers in the Class Structure*, Cambridge, University Press, Cambridge, 1985.

Perline, M. and V.R. Lorenz. "Factors Influencing Participation in Trade Union Activities," *American Journal of Economics and Sociology*, Vol. XXIII, 1978.

Perrow, C. and C. Jenkins. Insurgency of the Powerless: Farmworker's Movements (1946–1972). *American Sociological Review*, Vol. 42, April 1977.

Perry, D. "The Federal-Provincial Fiscal Arrangements Introduced in 1977." *Canadian Tax Journal*, Vol. XXV, No. 4, July - August 1977.

Pollert, Anna. *Girls, Wives, Factory Lives*. MacMillan, London, 1981.

Ponak, A. "Public Sector Dispute Resolution." *Relations Industrielle* Vol. 31, No. 4.

Porter, Marilyn. *Home, Work and Class Consciousness*. Manchester University Press, Manchester, 1983.

Prokop, U. "Production and the Context of Women's Daily Life." *New German Critique*, Number 13 (Winter) 1978.

Purcell, Kate. "Militancy and Acquiescence Amongst Women Workers," in Sandra Burman (ed.) *Fit Work for Women*, Croom Helm, 1979.

Reder, M. and George Neuman. "Conflict and Contract: The Use of Strikes," *Journal of Political Economy*, Vol. 88, No. 5, 1980.

Rickard, G. "The Effects of Financial Restraint on Health-Care." *Hospital Administration in Canada*, June, 1975.

Rowbotham, S. *Women's Consciousness, Man's World*, Harmondsworth, Penguin, 1974.

Sachs, K. "Engels Revisited: Women The Organization of Production and Private Property" in R. Reiter *Toward an Anthropology of Women*. New York, Monthly Review Press, 1975.

Salaman, G. *Working*. Ellis Horwood, Chichester, 1986.

———*Community and Occupation*, Cambridge University Press, Cambridge, 1974.

———*Work Organisations, Resistance and Control*, Longman, London, 1979.

———"Managing the Frontier of Control" in Giddens, Anthony and Mackenzie, Gavin (eds.), *Social Class and the Division of Labour*, Cambridge University Press, Cambridge, pp. 46–62.

Schreiner, J. "Hospital Staff Arbitration: Beginning New Labour Trend." *Financial Post*, May 18, 1983, p. 34.

Schutt, R.K. "Models of Militancy: Support for Strikes and Work Actions Among Public Employees." *Industrial and Labour Relations Review*, Vol. 35, No. 3, April 1982.

Seve, L. *Man in Marxist Theory and the Psychology of Personality*. Humanities Press, New Jersey,1978.

Sharpe, S. *Double Identity: The Lives of Working Mothers*. Penguin, 1984.

Shorter, E. and Tilly. *Strikes in France 1830–1968*. Cambridge University Press, London, 1974.

Smith, D. "Strikes in the Canadian Public Sector" in *Conflict or Compromise, The Future of Public Sector Industrial Relations*, G. Swimmer (ed.) Institute for Research on Public Policy.

Sniderman, P. and P. Tetlok. "Interrelationship of Political Ideology and Public Opinion."

Stevens, C. "Is Compulsory Arbitration Compatible with Bargaining," *Industrial Relations*, February 1966.

Stevenson, G. "Federalism and the Political Economy of the Canadian State" in *The Canadian State*. University of Toronto Press, Toronto, 1977.

Stinson, J. "Women in the Canadian Union of Public Employees." Unpublished Paper, Carleton University, Ottawa, 1978.

Stoddard, G. *The Privatization Debate, Issues and Policy Considerations*. A Research Project requested by Health and Welfare Canada, Ottawa, 1985.

Stoddard, G. "Rationalizing the Health Care System" in D. Conklin (ed.), *Ottawa and the Provinces: The Distribution of Money and Power*. Ontario Economic Council, Toronto, 1985.

Stone, C. "The Origins of Job Structures in the Steel Industry." Edwards et al, *Labour Market Segmentation*. Heath, Lexington, 1975.

Strauss, G. "The Union Government in the U.S." Research Past and Future," *Industrial Relations*, Vol. 16, No. 2, May 1977.

Stromberg, Ann H. and Shirley Harkness. *Women Working, Theories and Facts in Perspective*. Mayfield Publishing Company, New York, 1978.

Swartz, D. "The Politics of Reform: Conflict and Accommodation in Canadian Health Policy: in *The Canadian State*. University of Toronto Press, Toronto, 1977.

Swimmer, G. "Militancy in Public Sector Unions" in *Conflict or Compromise: The Future of Public Sector Industrial Relations*. Institute for Research on Public Policy.

Swindensky, Vandercamp. "A Micro-Econometric Analysis of Strike Activity in Canada." *Journal of Labour Research*, Vol. III, No. 4, Fall 1982.

Sykes, R. "The Squeeze is on in Ottawa" in *Proceedings of the Conference on Medicare: The Decisive Year*. Canadian Centre for Policy Alternatives, Montreal, 1982.

Thompson, M. and Gene Swimmer (ed.) *Conflict or Compromise, The Future of Public Sector Industrial Relations*. Institute for Research on Public Policy, Ottawa, 1984.

Thompson, Paul. *The Nature of Work*, Macmillan, London, 1985.

Timbrell, D. "Ontario's Attitude to Cost Restraint." *Hospital Administration Canada*, December, 1977.

Torrance, G. *The Underside of the Hospital*. Ph.D. dissertation, University of Toronto, 1978.

Trudeau, Right Honourable Pierre. "Established Program Financing: A Proposal Regarding the Major Cost Shared Programs in the Fields of Health and Post Secondary Education." Statement Tabled at the Federal-Provincial Cost-Sharing Conference, June, 1976.

Warner, M. and J. David Endelstein. *Comparative Union Democracy*. Wiley, N.Y., 1976.

Weiler, Joseph M. *Interest Arbitration, Measuring Justice in Employment*. The Carswell Company Limited, Toronto, 1981.

Weiler, P. *Arbitration Report: Between 65 Participating Hospitals and Canadian Union of Public Employees and Their Unions*, June 1, 1981.

———*Reconcilable Differences*. Carswell, Toronto, 1980.

Weldon, J. C. *Wage Controls and The Labour Movement*. Research Report No. 10, Canadian Centre for Policy Alternatives, (N.D.)

Westwood, S. *All Day, Everyday, Factory and Family in the Making of Women's Lives*. Pluto Press, London, 1984.

Wheeler, H.T. "How Compulsory Arbitration Affects Compromise," *Industrial Relations*, Vol. 17, No. 1, February 1978.

Whitaker, R. "Fighting the Cold War at Home" in Miliband et al. (ed.), *Socialist Register*. Merlin, London, 1984.

White, J.P. *Brief to the Board of the Hamilton General and Henderson Hospitals. Replacing the Registered Nursing Assistant: The Implications*, May, 1987.

————"Gender and Labour Process in the Determination of Public Sector Strike Activities," University of Western Ontario Discussion Series, London, February, 1986.

————"The 1981 Hospital Strike," *Workers and Their Communities Conference*, Ottawa, May, 1985.

————"Part-time Work and the Crisis in Nursing" in Lundy and Warme (ed.), *Part-time Work in Canada*. Prager, New York, (forthcoming).

————*Relativizing the Factors in the Nursing Crisis*. CAIS Working Papers 01–89, University of Western Ontario, 1989.

————"Compulsory Arbitration and Bargaining in Ontario Hospitals" in H. Jain (ed.) *Emerging Trends in Canadian Industrial Relations*. Canadian Industrial Relations Association, McMaster University, Hamilton, 1987.

White, Julie. *Women and Unions*. Canadian Advisory Council on the Status of Women, Ottawa, 1980.

Wipper, Audrey. *The Sociology of Work*. Carleton University Press, Ottawa, 1984.

Wirsig, C. "Wider Perspectives on Hospital Constraints." *Hospital Administration in Canada*. April, 1976.

Wolfe, D. "The State and Economic Policy in Canada 1968–75" in *The Canadian State*. Leo Panitch (ed.) University of Toronto Press, Toronto, 1977.

Wood, Stephen (ed.) *The Degradation of Work*. Hutchinson, London, 1982.

Yeandle, Susan. *Women's Working Lives, Patterns and Strategies*. Tavistock Publications, London, 1984.

Zald, M. and J. McCarthy. "Resource Mobilization Model." *American Journal of Sociology*, Vol. 82, No. 6, 1976.

Zimbalist, A. *Case Studies on the Labour Process*. Monthly Review, New York, 1979.

NEWSPAPERS

Financial Post, "Hospital Staff Arbitration: Beginning New Labor Trend?" J. Schreiner, 18 May 1963, p. 34.

————"Chronic Care for Hospital Strikers," 07 February 1981, p. 18.

Globe and Mail, "Hospital Workers Treated Unfairly," 17 April 1969.

————"56 Ontario Hospitals Facing Illegal Strike," 21 October 1978, p. 1.

————"55 (Ontario) Hospitals Seek Order from Labor Board to Stop Strike Vote," 23 October 1978, p. 14.

————"Canadian Union of Public Employees Hospitals Argue for Strike Ban Order," 28 October 1978, p. 5.

————"CUPE, 55 Hospitals Opt for Arbitration After Strike Vetoed," 30 October 1978, p. 1.

————"Unrest Grows at Hospitals," 8 February 1979, p. T1.

————"M.D. Assails Hospital Cutbacks After Sick Woman Dies at Home," 14 May 1979.

————"Canadian Union of Public Employees Chauvinists Amazed Grace Hartman is CUPE's Chief," 10 September 1979, p. B4.

————"Illegal Strike at Ontario Hospitals Put to Vote," 20 December 1980, p. 5.

————"Elgie to Set Arbitrator After Ontario Hospital Workers Union Boycott," 12 January 1981, p. 5.

————"Employees of Ontario Hospitals Want Strike—Union," 16 January 1981, p. 5.

————"Ontario Hospital Workers Back Illegal Strike," 19 January 1981, p. 5.

————"Court Rejects CUPE's Bid to Halt Probe of Hospital Strike," 20 January 1981, p. 2.

————"Hospital Union Told to Call Off Strike Plan," 22 January 1981, p. 1.

————"Canadian Union of Public Employees Ontario Labor Relations Bd. Hospital Union Told to Call Off (Ontario) Strike Plan," 22 January 1981, p. 1.

————"Illegal Ontario Hospital Workers Strike (Ed)," 23 January 1981, p. 6.

————"CUPE Begins Province-Wide Hospital Strike," 26 January 1981, p. 1.

————"Court Order Sought to End Ontario Hospital Workers' Strike," 27 January 1981, p. 1.

————"Court Order Sought to End Strike by Hospital Workers," 27 January 1981, pp. 1–2.

————"Hospitals Look for Ways to Beat Strike Problems," 28 January 1981, p. 5.

————"Judge Reserves His Ruling on Ending Ontario Hospital Strike," 29 January 1981, p. 1.

————"Hospitals Use Scare Tactics—Strikers," 29 January 1981, p. 5.

————"Ontario Hospital Association Hospitals Raise Offer on Eve of Strike Ruling," 30 January 1981, p. 5.

————"Ontario Hospital Association Offer to End Strike if Reprisals Dropped Refused by Hospitals," 02 February 1981, p. 1.

————"Hospital Strike a Clear Defeat, CUPE Leadership in Question," 04 February 1981, p. 5.

————"The Ontario Hospital Strike Victims," 04 February 1981, p. 5.

————"McMurtry Preparing Case Against Hartman," 05 February 1981, p. 4.

————"Lessons from Hospital Strike—Windsor," 12 February 1981, p. 7.

————"Weiler Named to Head Panel in CUPE Case," 14 February 1981, p. 5.

————"CUPE May Agree to Arbitration on Illegal Hospital Strike," 16 February 1981, p. 5.

———"Sudbury Hospitals Launch Reprisals for Illegal Strike," 18 February 1981, p. 24.

———"OFL Seeks Cash From Affiliates to Assist CUPE Hospital Strikers," 25 February 1981, p. 3.

———"OPP Approaching Papers in CUPE Hospital Strike Case," 13 March 1981, p. 3.

———"CUPE Chief Survives Attach by Workers Over Hospital Strike," 23 May 1981, p. 4.

———"Ontario Hospital Strike's Aftermath," 29 May 1981, p. 5.

———"Hartman Sentenced to 45 Days in Prison for Defying Court Injunction During Ontario Hospital Workers," 12 June 1981, p. 1.

———"Union Leader Hartman Won't Accept Day Parole," 16 June 1981, p. 11.

———"Government Hypocritical to Seek Raises Denied Labour—CUPE's Nicholson," 22 June 1981, p. 5.

———"Illegal Strikers not Protected Under Labor Law, Board Rules," 07 July 1981, p. 1.

———"Three Fired Workers Who Lead Strike Ordered Reinstated in Hamilton Hospital Ruling," 28 August 1981, p. 1.

———"Jailed for Illegal Hospital Walkout, Hartman Says She'd Back Another," 06 October 1981, p. 1.

———"CUPE Rejects General Strike as Protest Against Wage Controls," 10 October 1981, p. 11.

———"Decision on Strikers at Ontario Hospitals Reversed," 25 December 1981, p. 5.

———"Contempt Decision on Hospital Strikers Reversed," 25 December 1981, p. 5.

Halifax Chronicle-Herald, "Hartman Sentenced to 45-Day Jail Term," 12 June 1981, p. 4.

Hamilton Spectator, "30 Year Old Assumptions Hinder Industrial Relations," 31 January 1979, p. 3.

———"Arbitrators Lack Guts," July 4.

———"Hospitals Staff Urged to Reject Contract Offer," Friday, 24 October 1980, p. 10.

Kitchener-Waterloo Record, "Hospital Contract Leads to Feud Between Two Union Branches," 19 April 1979.

———CUPE Facing Uphill Struggle for 18% Hike," 04 July 1979.

Labour Review, "Unions Rally to Fight Hospital Reprisals (For Illegal Strike)," May/June 1981, p. 5.

London Free Press, "More Than Their Fair Share of the Inflation Burden," Saturday, 07 July 1979.

———"CUPE Leadership Floored Over Strikes at Hospitals," 03 April 1981.

———"CUPE Suffering from Severe Dry Rot Case," Thursday, 28 May 1983.

Montreal Gazette, "Weiler New Actor for Labour Stage—Finn," 22 November 1980, p. 19.

———"Hospital Staff Will Study Strike Action," 09 January 1981, p. 10.

————"Talks Resume in Ontario Hospital Strike," 28 January 1981, p. 2.

————"Hospital Strike Ruling Put Off," 29 January 1981, p. 10.

Ontario Labour, "Hospital Strike Debate Bitter," January/February 1982, p. 8.

Sunday Star, "Hospital Workers Vote for Illegal Strike Next Week," 18 January 1981, p. A3.

————"Give Employees Right to Strike—Nursing Home Operator," 24 May 1981, p. D23.

Toronto Star, "Grace Hartman Attacks British Columbia Law on Strikes in Public Sector," 24 October 1977, p. D11.

————"No Word on Banning Hospital Strike Vote," 28 October 1978, p. A3.

————"What is Really A Fair Wage," 11 July 1979.

————"Hospital Union Leaders Plan to Battle Proposed Settlement," 20 October 1980, p. A39.

————"Labor Board Told It Can Halt Strike at Hospitals," 20 January 1981, p. A3,

————"Don't Strike Union Orders Hospital Staff," 22 January 1981, p. A1.

————"Union Defies Order to Halt Hospital Strike," 24 January 1981, p. A1.

————"Defiant Workers Strike Hospitals," 26 January 1981, p. A1.

————"Strikers Tightening Blockade on Hospitals," 27 January 1981, p. A1.

————"Judge Delays Ruling on Strikers," 29 January 1981, p. A1.

————"Judge Orders End to Strike," 30 January 1981, p. A1.

————"Strikers Defiant as Talks Fail; Arbitration Call—But Hospital Pickets Stay," 31 January 1981, p. A1.

————"Hospital Strike 'Turning Point'—Morton," 02 February 1981, p. A8.

————"8-Day Hospital Strike Ends as it Began—In Bitterness," 03 February 1981, p. A1.

————"Hospital Strike Failed But Still Poses Hard Questions," 04 February 1981, p. A10.

————"4 Strikers Fired 40 Suspended at Toronto Western," 12 February 1981, p. A3.

————"Strikers Put CUPE Out of Business," 06 June 1981, p. A13.

————"3 Among Fired Hospital Strikers Win Jobs Back," 28 August 1981, p. A16.

————"CUPE Faces Future With No Strike Fund," 06 October 1981, p. A3.

————"Union is Not 'A Paper Tiger'—Hartman," 04 November 1981, p. A9.

Vancouver Sun, "CUPE Leader Hartman Attacks Right-to-Work 'Lunatic Fringe'," 16 June 1978, p. B1.

————"CUPE's Hartman Jailed," 12 June 1981, p. G10.

Winnipeg Free Press, "CUPE Leader Hartman Says Public Thinks Unions Feed Inflation," 25 May 1981, p. 12.

————"Hartman Acclaimed to fourth term as CUPE President," 8 October 1981, p. 1.

GOVERNMENT DOCUMENTS

Arthurs, H. *Task Force on Labour Relations: Labour Disputes in Essential Industries*. Toronto, 1968.

Brown, D.M. *Task Force on Labour Relations: Interest Arbitration*. Toronto, 1968.

Canada, Government of. *Federal-Provincial Tax Structure Report*. Queens Printer, Ottawa: 1966.

——Canada, Government of. *The Federal Deficit in Perspective*. Department of Finance, 1983.

Canada Year Book, Statistics Canada, 1969–1980.

Hall, Emmett. *Canada's National-Provincial Health Programs for the 1980s*. Government of Canada, 1979.

Ontario, Government of. *Report of the Royal Commission on Compulsory Arbitration*. The Bennet Commission, Toronto, 1964.

——*The Impact of the Ontario Hospital Labour Disputes Arbitration Act, 1965: A Statistical Analysis*. Department of Labour, Research Branch. Toronto, 1970(a).

——*Selected Aspects of the Health Care Sector in Ontario*, Toronto, 1970(b).

——*The Effect of Fiscal Constraints on Hospital Employees*. Ministry of Health, Toronto, 1974(a).

——*Report of the Health Planning Task Force*. Ministry of Health. Toronto, 1974(b).

——*The Report of the Hospital Inquiry Commission*. (The Johnston Commission). Ministry of Health, Toronto, 1974.

——*The Report of the Special Program Review*. (Henderson Report). Ministry of the Treasury, Toronto, 1975.

——*Supplementary Actions to the 1975 Budget*. Ministry of the Treasury, Toronto, 1975.

——*Report of The Joint Advisory Committee of the Government of Ontario and the Ontario Medical Association on Methods to Control Costs*. Toronto, 1977.

——*Hospital Statistics*. No. 83–232, 1977, 1978(a).

——*Guidelines for Hospital Nursing Departments*, Toronto, 1978(b).

——*Hospital Labour Disputes Arbitration Act* (Revised 1980). Queen's Printer, Toronto, 1980.

——*Statement by the Honourable Larry Grossman, Minister of Health to the Committee on Social Development*. Toronto, 1982(a).

——*Final Report of the Task Force to Review Primary Health Care*. (Mustard Report). Ministry of Health, Toronto, 1982(b).

——*Health Care: The 1980s and Beyond*. Toronto, 1983.

——*Hansard Official Report of Debates*. June, 1984.

Province of Ontario. *Report of the Select Committee on Health Care Financing and Costs*. (McCafferey Report) October 17, 1978.

Saskatchewan, Government of. Social Services Department Federal-Provincial E.P.F. Briefing Notes, 1976.

Statistics Canada. *Corporations and Labour Unions Returns Act*, Part II, Labour Unions Annual 71–202.

Weiler, P. *Task Force on Labour Relations: Labour Arbitration and Industrial Change*, Toronto, 1968.

MISCELLANEOUS PRIMARY RESEARCH MATERIAL

CUPE Correspondence, Minutes of Meetings, Internal Reviews and Selected Bargaining Documents

Correspondence

CUPE to Service Employees International Union October 16, 22, November 17 and 22, 1977.
Peter Douglas to Hospital Local Presidents, February 2, 1980.
Peter Douglas to P. O'Keeffe, February 15, 1980.
P. O'Keeffe to CUPE Ontario Division, March 5, 1980.
K. Cummings to P. Douglas, March 16, 1980.
Dufresne to Hartman, March 25, 1980.
Gilbert Levine to J. MacMillan, October 2, 1980.
P. O'Keeffe to CUPE Ontario Division, October 8, 1980.
Justin Legault to Grace Hartman, October 23, 1980.
McQuarrie to G. Hartman, October 30, 1980.
G. Hartman to G. Levine and J. MacMillan, November 3, 1980.
C. Dufresne to P. Douglas, November 30, 1980.
Len Lawrence to Striking CUPE members, Regulations for Strikers, St. Peters Hospital (Hamilton) to CUPE members, n.a., February 6, 1981.
W. Noonan to Miss Grange, February 11, 1981.
Mayor Powell to Sister Joan O'Sullivan, February 23, 1981.
Mayor Powell to K. Dixon, February 24, 1981.
Ontario Hospital Bargaining Review Committee to Ontario Hospital Locals, November 3, 1981.
O'Keeffe to Ontario Staff Representatives, December 1, 1981.
Middleton to Douglas, December 16, 1981.
Ontario Hospital Bargaining Review Committee to Ontario Hospital Locals, March 15, 1982.
P. O'Keeffe Personal Statement to CUPE Members, A Rebuttal, 1981.
P. O'Keeffe to CUPE Ontario, May 6, 1982.

Official Documents

Grievance Arbitration N. Train, M. Harrington, M. Martin award (K. Swan Chairman).
Memorandum of Agreement between Participating Local Unions of CUPE and Participating Hospitals, September 26, 1980.
Arbitration Award in the matter of the HLDAA, between sixty-five hospitals and the CUPE and Local Unions (Swan Arbitration), June 1, 1981.

Ontario Council of Hospital Unions. *Bylaws of the Ontario Council of Hospital Unions, Canadian Union of Public Employees,* February, 1982.

———Minutes: Founding Convention of the Ontario Council of Hospital Unions, March 31 to April 2, 1982.

Minutes

Minutes of the Health Care Workers' Coordinating Committee Meetings: December 5, 6, 1978; February 13, 16; March 14, 1979.
Objectives and Bylaws, February 1980.
"Report On Structure," February 1980.
Minutes: National Executive Board Meeting, 1981.

Miscellaneous

Progressive Action Campaign; Prepare for a Strike, November, 1980.
Report to the 1981 Health Care Workers Conference from the Central Bargaining Committee, 1981.
Vincer Commission, *Examination and Review: Hospital Workers Negotiations,* April, 1982.

CUPE—OHA Correspondence, Bargaining Materials and OHA Bulletins

Dixon to Hamilton Civic Hospital CUPE Members Dissuading Strike Action, January 22, 1981.
OHA to CUPE Local 1144, May 5, 1979.
OHA *For Your Information* (Internal Bulletin)
Volume 12, No. 6, March 15, 1978
Volume 13, No. 3, January 31, 1979
No. 4, February 15, 1979
No. 5, February 28, 1979
Peter Douglas to George Campbell; January 17, March 13 and March 17, 1978.

Miscellaneous Documents Cited

F. Anderson to Minister of Health n.d. 1979.
Anti-Inflation Board to Ron Bass, OHA, August 1978.
College of Nurses of Ontario, "RNA Questionnaire: Excellent Response," College Communique, Vol. 7, Number 3, May 1982.
John Holt (Local 1605) to Minister of Health, June 21, 1979.
Ontario Labour Relations Board, Cease and Desist.
Order Ajax and Pickering General Hospital et al. and William Brown et al., January 23, 1981.
Transcripts of Termination Arbitrations, St. Peters Hospital Employees, April 23–24, 1981.

Union Newsletters, Policy Statements, Union Journals and Miscellaneous Leaflets

Anonymous "The Hospital Revolutionaries" n.d. (January 1981).

CUPE, "Brief to Ministry of Labour Condemning the Hospital Labour Disputes Arbitration Act." C.U.P.E., 1971(b).

CUPE, "Central Bargain Committee Report to the 1981 Health-Care Workers' Conference," 1981.

CUPE, *The Facts*, Vol. I, #5, 7, 8, 9, 10 (1979); Vol. II, #3, 4, 5, 9 (1980); Vol. III, #1, 2, 7, 8 (1981); Vol. VI, #3 (1984)

CUPE, *The Ontario Hospital Worker*

"Vote No Out October 27, 1980" n.d.

"Regional Executive Urges Rejection of Settlement," n.d.

"Petition" November 6, 1980

CUPE *Policy Statement on the Action Program for* CUPE Convention Documents, 1979.

CUPE *The Public Employee*

"How Do I Comfort a Child: The Recline in Standards of Health Care," Spring, 1981.

CUPE, "Report on Structure and Bargaining for C.U.P.E. Ontario Hospital Workers." February, 1982.

CUPE, *The Status of Women in* CUPE, Ottawa, 1971(a).

CUPE, Union Local 778, "The right to Grieve Suspensions," n.d.

CUPE, Union Local "Retribution at the Perley" n.d.

CUPE, Union Reports on Suspensions and Dismissals at Henderson Hospital n.d.

Ontario Council of Hospital Workers, *The Hospital Worker*, No. 8, September 1986.

Ontario Federation of Labour, "Pilkey Says Law Criminal Not Workers," *Information*, January 28, 1981.

SEIU Local 220, "Highlights" June 29, 1979.

Strike Bulletin #1, n.d., #2 (January 28, 1981), #3 (January 29, 1981), #4 (January 19, 1981), #5 n.d., #6 n.d., #7 (February 1, 1981).

Westernews: February, April, May, July, August, October, December 1979; March, September, October, December 1980.

Index